Union Public

D0114326

FERGUSON
CAREER BIOGRAPHIES

ALTHEA
GIBSON
Tennis Player

Michael Benson

Ferguson
An imprint of ☑ Facts On File

Althea Gibson: Tennis Player

Copyright © 2006 by Facts On File, Inc.

Ferguson
An imprint of Facts On File, Inc.
132 West 31st Street
New York NY 10001

Library of Congress Cataloging-in-Publication Data

Benson, Michael
  Althea Gibson : tennis player / Michael Benson
    p. cm.
  Includes index.
  ISBN 0-8160-5889-X (hc : alk. paper)
 1. Gibson, Althea, 1927—Juvenile literature. 2. Tennis players—United States—
Biography—Juvenile literature. 3. African American women tennis players—
Biography—Juvenile literature. I. Title.
  GV994.G53B46 2006
  796.342´092—dc22
                                                                2005007916

Ferguson books are available at special discounts when purchased in bulk quantities for businesses, associations, institutions, or sales promotions. Please call our Special Sales Department in New York at (212) 967-8800 or (800) 322-8755.

You can find Ferguson on the World Wide Web at http://www.fergpubco.com

Text design by David Strelecky

Pages 113–126 adapted from Ferguson's *Encyclopedia of Careers and Vocational Guidance, Thirteenth Edition*

Printed in the United States of America

MP Hermitage 10 9 8 7 6 5 4 3 2 1

This book is printed on acid-free paper.

CONTENTS

1 Growing Up · 1

2 Early Days on the Courts · 13

3 From Forest Hills to Wimbledon · 35

4 Goodwill Tour · 49

5 America's Outstanding Female Athlete · 67

6 A New Sport · 81

7 Time to Teach · 93

Time Line · 109

How to Become a Professional Athlete · 113

To Learn More about Professional
    Athletes   **125**

To Learn More about Althea Gibson
    and Tennis   **127**

Tennis Glossary   **131**

Index   **135**

1

GROWING UP

On August 25, 1927, Althea Gibson was born in the small town of Silver, South Carolina. She entered the world at, as she later put it, a "solid eight pounds."

Her mother would later tell Althea, "You were what you call a big, fat one."

Althea was the first-born child of Daniel and Annie Gibson, who were sharecroppers. They lived on and tended to a five-acre cotton farm, but they did not own it. They paid the farm's owner with a percentage of the crop and sold the remainder of the cotton to buy food and keep the farm running. Until Althea was three, she lived in a small cabin with her mother, father, and one uncle.

Daniel said Silver was a "three-store" town, bigger than the one-store towns but not that big. Both of Althea's parents were large, strong people who were used to hard work. Annie enjoyed riding the farm animals. If a horse wasn't available, she'd ride a cow or a pig instead.

Growing Up During the Great Depression

Times were tough during Althea's childhood, especially when bad weather caused the cotton crops to fail for three years in a row. To make matters worse, this was the time of the Great Depression in the United States. Almost everyone was poor and prices were very low. The cotton that the farm did produce sold for very little money. During their last year in South Carolina, the Gibsons made only $75. Althea's family decided to move north, where they hoped they would find opportunities.

However, they couldn't afford to move all at once. Althea's Aunt Sally Washington—her mother's sister—lived in New York, and Althea went to live with her when she was three.

Althea's father came north next and looked for work. When he quickly found a job as a handyman, he arranged for his wife to join him and Althea. All three of the Gibsons lived with Aunt Sally in Harlem, an African-American neighborhood in Manhattan.

In addition to this being the time of the Depression, it was also the time of prohibition in the United States. Under prohibition, selling and drinking alcoholic beverages was illegal. Until 1933, when prohibition ended, Aunt Sally made money by selling illegal (bootleg) liquor out of her Harlem apartment.

Althea grew up around a lot of drinking and often saw her uncles and their friends drunk. They would even give liquor to Althea, who was drunk on whiskey more than once before she was old enough to go to school.

Not wanting their daughter to grow up in this unhealthy environment, Althea's mother and father sent her to live with another aunt, Daisy Kelly, in Philadelphia.

Mischief-Maker

By this time Althea often refused to do as she was told. To put it mildly, Aunt Daisy found her to be quite a handful. Althea got her clothes dirty, fought with boys, and seemed always to be getting into mischief.

When Althea was nine, she was sent back to New York to live with her mother and father. By this time, however, Daniel and Annie had managed to get their own apartment, on West 143rd Street in Harlem.

As Althea later put it, the story of her youth "wasn't all pretty." She continued to be a problem. She simply did not like being told what to do.

In the meantime, Althea grew and grew. She became very tall and strong, standing close to six feet. She was queen of the playground. When neighborhood children were playing a game or a sport, the chances were good that Althea was better at it than anyone else.

Althea and her parents, Annie and Daniel (Corbis)

It was after Althea returned to New York and her family had their own apartment that she began, as she put it, "getting into real trouble." She skipped school frequently, missing more school than she attended.

Truancy had always been a problem for Althea. Even when she was little she skipped school. Once, she was caught and spanked right in the classroom. Now the problem was more severe, and Althea was missing weeks of school at a time.

Her father's solution was to give her frequent whippings, but this only sent the little girl to the local police precinct where she told police that she feared going home because her father was beating her.

In addition to skipping school, she began to steal. She and her friends called it "snitching." Most of it involved sneaking into movies and taking fruit from fruit stands without paying, but there were signs that the "snitching" problem was getting worse. One time, she stole a bike and sold it.

Afraid of being beaten for her bad behavior, Althea would stay away from home for days at a time. Eventually Daniel realized that whipping his daughter was not going to improve her behavior.

Althea was convinced that her father had wanted a son but instead he got her. He treated her as much like a boy as he could get away with. Daniel signed her up for boxing lessons. His plan was twofold. For one thing, he thought that as she grew to her full adult size, she could become a professional-quality boxer, and there was money to be made in those days in women's boxing. Plus, since Althea seemed determined to live on the streets, Daniel figured she should learn to defend herself. She learned to stand up to bullies—and became a very good boxer, very quickly.

Althea never really wanted to fight professionally, and Daniel soon gave up on the dream. Still, it wasn't long before her ability to duck and throw a punch came in handy.

Street-Fighting Girl

On one occasion, Althea was going to visit her Aunt Sally when she came across one of her uncles surrounded by a local gang called the Sabres. Her uncle seemed slightly drunk and the gang was in the process of robbing him.

The little girl came to her uncle's defense. One of the gang members threw a sharpened screwdriver at her, cutting her on the hand. Althea dragged her uncle into the apartment building. She then went back out to get the boy who had cut her.

The two had a fight that, according to Althea, went up one side of the block and down the other. Although there was no clear-cut winner—both were bloodied and bruised—Althea gained the respect of the gang. None of the Sabres bothered her or members of her family again.

It was a couple of years later, after her boxing lessons, that Althea became a legend in her neighborhood. It happened when Althea had a street fight after school. With a huge crowd gathered to watch, Althea ended the fight against the girl who had challenged her with one punch.

After learning of Althea's one-punch knockout, nobody on 143rd Street was quick to bother her.

Trophies and Medals

Althea may have been a good fighter, but she didn't like to fight. She did it to protect herself, or her family, but not for fun. There were plenty of other games to play that were more fun, and Althea was good at them all.

She still didn't like to go to school, but now instead of snitching she preferred to spend her days in the playground playing baseball or basketball.

Basketball was her favorite sport. She and her best friends could be found on the playground for hours each day. They would play any kind of game. If there were just two of them, they would play one-on-one. If a couple of others showed up, boys or girls, they'd play two-on-two. After playing all day and much of the night, they would go to a cheap restaurant for plates of collard greens and rice.

Sometimes, if she had money, she would go to the bowling alley. By the time she was 12, she had gathered a shelf full of trophies and medals from city-sponsored competitions she had won.

And sometimes she would have great adventures. One time, when she was about 12, she and her friend scrounged for soda bottles to return for the deposit and made enough money to rent a bike. They then rode the bike from Harlem to the World's Fair, which was in Flushing-Meadow Park, 10 miles away in the New York

City borough of Queens. After a full day at the park, they rode the bike back to Harlem and returned it.

Even though Althea had missed so much time in school, in 1941 she managed to graduate from junior high school. She was sent to high school at the Yorkville Trade School. She found the sewing classes interesting for a year or so but then began to skip school as much as ever. Wanted for truancy, she again was afraid to go home.

Instead, Althea rode the subway all night long. It was a place where she could sit and doze and be out of the weather. She was a homeless teenager until she learned of a place called the Society for the Prevention of Cruelty to Children—the SPCC. Althea learned that kids who had no place to go could stay there. And they did take her in. She was given a bed to sleep in and a solid meal. As she recalled, "It was a lot better than riding the subway."

The next morning, a lady at the SPCC called Daniel Gibson and reported that his daughter was there. Daniel whipped Althea with a strap when he got her home, and she ran away again. Althea told the people at the SPCC what had happened. She showed them the welts that were still on her back. The home took her in once again, and this time they didn't call her father to pick her up.

She lived at the SPCC for a time and then her father took her back, agreeing not to beat her anymore. Althea refused to return to high school, so she got her working papers. She took a few night classes and worked at a series of jobs.

She was a counter girl at a restaurant. She was a messenger for a blueprint company. She worked in a button factory and a dress factory. She ran an elevator at the Dixie Hotel. (Back in those days, elevators weren't automatic. You had to tell the operator which floor you were going to and then he or she would "drive" the elevator to that floor.) She also cleaned chickens in a butcher shop. Her favorite job was sorting mail at a school, but she lost it when she got caught skipping work to go to the movies.

First Brush with Tennis

During the summer after junior high, Althea learned a game called paddle tennis, which she played on a city street. Because Harlem was too crowded to have enough playgrounds for all its residents, the city had blocked off some streets to traffic to serve as play areas. One such block was the one where Althea lived. Almost right outside her door the city had set up paddle tennis courts. Paddle tennis was played with a paddle (like table tennis, also known as ping pong) and on a court that was about half the size of a regulation tennis court. Althea quickly learned that she was very good at paddle tennis.

She became her neighborhood paddle-tennis champion. She then played the champions from other neighborhoods

Althea, with her natural athleticism, displayed a talent for tennis from the first time she picked up a racket. (Associated Press)

and won those matches, too. Her collection of trophies and ribbons grew. She held on to those treasures for the rest of her life.

It was while playing paddle tennis that Althea was "discovered." The man who discovered Althea was a Harlem musician named Buddy Walker. Buddy was known as "Harlem's Society Orchestra Leader." He worked mostly weekends, and during the week he was a volunteer "play leader" on Althea's block. He was on duty when Althea was badly beating a friend at a game of paddle tennis. Walker could see how talented the girl was.

Buddy figured that if Althea was this good at paddle tennis, she would also be very good at regular tennis. He also figured that the game of tennis could lead Althea to bigger and better things. So Buddy bought two second-hand tennis rackets and took Althea to Harlem's Mount Morris Park, where there was a wall against which tennis balls could be hit.

Just as Buddy had expected, Althea hit the ball with the force of a grown man, and she could make it go wherever she wanted.

2

EARLY DAYS
ON THE
COURTS

Buddy Walker was very excited about Althea's skill. He soon took her to the Harlem River Tennis Courts, where she would play her first real tennis matches. Buddy brought along a friend who was a good tennis player. As Althea volleyed with the friend, her skills were so apparent that other games stopped, and everyone watched Althea play.

Among those spectators was schoolteacher Juan Serrill, a member of the New York's top African-American tennis club, the Cosmopolitan Club. According to Althea, the Cosmopolitan was "*the* ritzy tennis club in Harlem."

The Cosmopolitan Club

In those days all of the major tennis tournaments in the world were for whites only. They were sponsored by whites-only country clubs. There were only a few African-American clubs, such as the Cosmopolitan Club, where members could play tennis.

The American Tennis Association (ATA) organized and ran tennis tournaments for African-American players. However, many young black athletes in those days, who might have become great tennis players, chose other sports instead.

Just as there were no baseball leagues in which blacks and whites played together, there were no integrated tennis tournaments. Whites played with whites, blacks with blacks, and the white players received all of the fame.

It was a "fact of life." Blacks "weren't allowed" to play tennis. Most African Americans couldn't afford to play even if they were allowed.

For these reasons, black clubs like the Cosmopolitan Club were eager to find young, talented black tennis players and help promote tennis as a sport that African Americans could play.

Juan Serrill arranged for Althea to visit the club and to volley (hit the ball back and forth over the net) with the club professional, Fred Johnson. She performed so well that the members of the club passed the hat and put together enough money to buy Althea a club membership. Fred Johnson, who had only one arm, became Althea's new tennis teacher.

Althea saw Mr. Johnson, as she called him, a couple of times a week. He taught her not just how to play tennis but how to *think* tennis. She learned *why* she should strike the ball in a certain way, in addition to learning how to do it. She learned to think ahead, to know what her opponent was going to do before she did it.

Althea was a quick learner on the tennis court when it came to playing the game. She was slower to learn the rules of behavior that went along with the sport. Tennis was a formal sport in which the players were expected to dress and act in a certain manner.

Fred Johnson, Althea's first tennis coach, taught her how to think and play like a professional tennis player. (Time Life Pictures/Getty Images)

While playing tennis at the Cosmopolitan Club, Althea became friends with Mrs. Rhoda Smith, a member of the club who, 10 years before, had lost her own daughter. Mrs. Smith, as Althea recalled, "practically adopted" her.

Mrs. Smith bought Althea her tennis clothes, which were always white in those days.

Mrs. Smith later told the press, "I was the first woman Althea ever played tennis with, and she resented it because I was always trying to improve her ways. I kept saying 'Don't do this,' and 'Don't do that,' and sooner or later she would holler, 'Mrs. Smith, you're always pickin' on me.' I guess I was, too, but I had to. When a loose ball rolled onto her court, she would simply bat it out of the way in any direction at all instead of politely sending it back to the player it belonged to, as is done in tennis. But Althea had played in the street all her life and she just didn't know any better."

On the court, Althea slowly became a more polite and respectful person. Off the court, however, she was as wild as ever. She worked a series of jobs for little money, but eventually stopped working, left the SPCC, and returned home. She still found living with her parents very unpleasant and spent her days and many of her nights on the streets. She was eventually picked up by the New York City welfare department and sent to live with a foster family.

Despite all of this, she continued her tennis lessons at the Cosmopolitan Club. Tennis provided the only stability in her life, the only part of her life that offered her self-esteem.

When Althea was 14, she got to see one of the world's best women tennis players in action, champion Alice Marble. It happened not long after Althea started taking tennis lessons from Fred Johnson. Alice, who had won major championships in England and in the United States, came to the Cosmopolitan Club to play an exhibition match. Althea carefully watched the way the champion played. She was greatly inspired by Marble's power and aggressiveness. Althea loved the way Alice charged the nets and took her opponent's shots head on. Althea decided she wanted nothing more than to play tennis the way Alice Marble did, like the best female tennis players in the world.

First Championship

During Althea's first year of playing tennis at the Cosmopolitan Club, some members did not approve of her. Althea's behavior was off-putting to several members of Harlem society. The problem was not that Althea was arrogant or stuck on herself. Quite the opposite was true. She was insecure. She was shy.

"I don't let many people get close to me," Althea said. To cover up, she acted cocky.

The Cosmopolitan Club members appreciated Althea's potential as a tennis player but were embarrassed by her behavior off the court. But feelings within the club toward

Althea improved greatly after her first year of lessons. That was when Althea had her first successes.

During the summer of 1942, Fred Johnson entered Althea in her first tournament. It was the New York State Open, an all-black event sanctioned by the ATA. Althea made the Cosmopolitan Club proud by winning the tournament.

Later that summer, she entered the ATA United States girl's championship, held at Lincoln University in Pennsylvania. She came in second place, losing to Nana Davis in the finals.

After the match, Davis let it be known that she didn't think much of Althea. Apparently some fans had heckled Althea during the final match. When the match was over and she had lost, she did not shake hands with her opponent as was expected but instead ran into the grandstand and insisted that the hecklers be ejected.

Years later, Nana recalled that match for a reporter: "Althea was a very crude creature. She had the idea she was better than anybody. I can remember her saying, 'Who's this Nana Davis? Let me at her.' And after I beat her, she headed straight for the grandstand without bothering to shake hands. Some kid had been laughing at her and she was going to throw him out."

Seeing that Althea needed some tennis lessons that had nothing to do with forehands and backhands, Mrs. Rhoda

Smith continued to teach Althea the do's and don'ts of tennis behavior.

Althea had plenty of time to learn. Like many other things in America, all ATA tournaments were canceled in 1943 because of World War II.

By the time Althea played in her next tournaments, in 1944, her behavior was perfect. Her play was near perfect as well. She won the girl's division ATA title in 1944 and successfully defended her crown in 1945.

A few weeks after World War II ended, in August 1945, Althea had her 18th birthday. She was now legally an adult. She had been receiving welfare money from the government because she was a minor, but now those checks stopped coming.

Althea worked as a waitress to make money and moved in with her friend Gloria Nightingale, who still lived at home with her family. Althea and Gloria both liked to stay out late, either playing basketball or going to a Harlem bowling alley.

The young women played together on a basketball team called The Mysterious Five. They played in a league and would play up to five games a week. Gloria and Althea would go to the bowling alley after the games, which were played at night. It was often three or four in the morning before they got home.

Sugar Ray

It was while bowling one night that Althea met a man whose influence would change her life. He was a boxer named Ray Robinson, nicknamed "Sugar Ray." Ray Robinson would go on to become one of the greatest boxers of all time, winning five world championships during his career. But in 1945, when he met Althea, he was simply a very talented contender fighting as a welterweight, who enjoyed bowling with his wife, Edna Mae.

"So you're Sugar Ray Robinson," Althea said when meeting the boxer. "Well I can beat you bowling right now."

The Robinsons quickly learned that Althea was a talented athlete who was struggling with life. They took the young girl under their wing. Her relationship with the Robinsons gave Althea some much-needed self-esteem.

Althea later said that she "worshiped" Robinson.

"It wasn't just because he was a wonderful fellow," Althea said, "and good to me when there was no special reason for him to be, it was because he was somebody, and I was determined that I was going to be somebody, too—if it killed me."

Althea recalled, "When Ray went into the army, I stayed with Edna a lot. I was what you might call her Girl Friday. I did everything I could to make our relationship a lasting one. When Ray was in training [for a boxing match], I used

Althea and her mentor, boxing legend Sugar Ray Robinson
(Corbis)

to go and live with Edna in a place on the other side of the mountain from his camp at Greenwood Lake, New York."

Althea and Edna would go for long hikes every day. It was six miles just to get to Ray's cabin and back.

"That wonderful mountain air seemed great to a kid from 143rd Street," Althea later said.

When Althea told Ray she wanted to learn how to play the saxophone, Ray offered to buy one for her. She found one in a pawnshop for $125 and Ray bought it. She kept the sax for the rest of her life but rarely played it.

"Which is a break for the neighbors," she would say.

Having turned 18, Althea could no longer compete in the girls' division in ATA tournaments. She moved up to the women's division, where the competition was tougher.

In her first women's division national tournament, in 1946, Althea made it all the way to the finals but lost to Roumania Peters. She chalked up her loss to overconfidence. She had been so used to winning that she had been caught, as Sugar Ray would have put it, "with her guard down" when she had to play a tough opponent.

Drs. Eaton and Johnson

Althea did not win the 1946 ATA National Championships, but she did get the attention of a pair of doctors among the spectators. They were Hubert A. Eaton and

Robert W. Johnson, and they were interested in promoting black tennis by developing young talented players.

The doctors approached Althea after her match and offered to put her through college while she developed her tennis game. Althea was forced to confess that she had dropped out of high school.

The doctors came up with a new plan. Althea could spend the school year with Dr. Eaton's family in North Carolina and attend a local school. During the summer she would move in with Dr. Johnson's family in Virginia and compete in ATA tournaments.

At first Althea did not want to go. She was afraid of the racism in the South, but the Robinsons told her this was an opportunity of a lifetime. So in August 1946, Althea took a train to Wilmington, North Carolina—Dr. Eaton's hometown.

Living in a Mansion

Althea's fears about being in the South subsided a bit when she was taken from the airport to the Eaton home in a big car with a chauffeur. Her new home, it turned out, was more like a mansion. There was a full-time maid and a private tennis court out on the lawn.

The Eatons purchased new clothes for Althea, and she received a weekly allowance. She was also expected to obey the household rules, which were the same for her as for the Eatons' children. She took an aptitude test and it was decided that she should re-start school—at Williston Industrial High School—in the 10th grade.

Along with her classes, she played saxophone in the band, sang in the choir, and was captain of the girls' basketball team. Her stint in the choir was short-lived. She quit after her deep voice got her placed with boys in the tenor section, a move that caused the other girls to tease her mercilessly. Developing a social life was tough for Althea, as she was four years older than the other kids in her class.

Even though she quit the school choir, she continued singing. She joined a jazz group made up of senior boys, and they played professionally on weekends in Wilmington nightclubs. Althea's first romance was with the group's trumpet player.

The Truth about the South

Although Althea's home life was luxurious, some of her fears about the South turned out to be true. When she rode the bus, she had to sit in the back. At some restaurants she was not allowed to dine at all. In others there was a special "Colored Only" section.

Black people had their own hospitals, schools, and playgrounds. Whites and blacks passed each other on the street but for the most part lived in separate worlds. That was the law in the South, and it made Althea feel ashamed.

Althea was pretty good about obeying the Eaton family rules, with one big exception. Once, when the family was out, she took the family car and drove around town in it. Someone saw her and told Dr. Eaton. When confronted, Althea confessed. Dr. Eaton said he would not punish her this time but that she could never pull such a stunt again—and she didn't.

Playing against, and with, Men

Althea did well in her studies, and her tennis game continued to get better. To test the limits of Althea's abilities, Dr. Eaton arranged for her to play against male tennis players. Men offered the best competition, and Althea still won far more matches than she lost.

When the 1946–47 school year was over, she moved to Virginia to live with the Johnsons. The truth was that she didn't spend that much time at home. Dr. Johnson, Althea, and a few other tennis players spent most of the summer in his car traveling from tournament to tournament. Althea competed both in women's singles and mixed doubles. Mixed doubles are teams made up of one man and one woman. Althea played mixed doubles with Dr. Johnson as her partner. Althea traveled to nine tournaments that year and won 17 times, nine in singles and eight in mixed doubles.

Her final victory of the summer was the 1947 ATA Women's National Championship—the first of her 10 ATA National Championships. It was the first time she had won a tournament in which reporters were present. Her victory was even mentioned in the *New York Times*.

"How would you like to play at Forest Hills?"

Although Althea dreamed of one day being the best female tennis player in the world, black or white, she didn't believe it would actually happen. The social wall between her and the world of white tennis seemed much too high to climb and too thick to bust through.

During the summer of 1948, Dr. Eaton asked her, "How would you like to play at Forest Hills?" She thought he was kidding. Forest Hills, New York, was where the U.S. National Championships were played.

Dr. Eaton explained that he was serious. Officials of the ATA had decided that they had the key that would open the door to integrated tennis—and that key was Althea.

"I'm ready any time they are," Althea said.

So, as Althea began her senior year of high school, ATA officials petitioned the United States Lawn Tennis

Association (USLTA) to allow Althea to play in their pre-
viously white-only tournaments. The USLTA said okay.
Althea could play in the Eastern Indoor Championships.
That tournament was held in Harlem, in the 143rd Street
Armory.

The Armory was a huge building. It had formerly been
used by the army for storage but had been replaced by a
new facility. The old Armory was now used for sporting
events such as indoor track meets and tennis—and it was
only blocks away from where Althea had grown up.

Indoor events were easier to integrate since they were
played in public arenas. Outdoor events were held in
white-only country clubs, so club rules had to be changed
before an African American could play.

Thirty-two women were entered in the tournament.
Althea won her first two matches to make it to the final
eight. She then played Betty Rosenquest in the quarterfinals but lost 8-6, 6-0.

Althea was disappointed, but she wasn't disgraced,
either. Her performance had been good enough to get her
invited to the National Indoor Championships the next
week.

Again, Althea made it to the final eight before losing,
this time to Nancy Chaffee. Althea had proven that she
belonged with America's elite women tennis players—
black or white.

College Life

In June 1949, Althea graduated tenth in her class from Williston Industrial High School. She was offered a full scholarship to attend Florida A&M University in Tallahassee to play tennis. Florida A&M was one of the country's largest all-black colleges.

That summer Althea won all of the ATA tournaments she entered. She tried to enter the outdoor USLTA tournaments held that summer, but she was refused. The outdoor tournaments were held at private country clubs that forbade black people from playing there.

Althea was not personally involved in the struggle to integrate the outdoor USLTA tournaments. Getting ready for college in the fall and playing in the ATA tournaments was enough to keep her occupied. She allowed the ATA to fight the integration battle for her.

Althea had gotten her idea of what college life was like from the movies. When she got to Florida A&M in the fall of 1949, she was disappointed. Between the school rules on campus and segregation off campus, Althea felt restless.

She had to sign out and give her destination each time she left campus. Because she was a freshman, she had to be back on campus by 9:00 P.M. Seniors got to stay off campus until 11:00 P.M., which wasn't much better as far as Althea was concerned. She loved late nights.

There was little for her to do except study and play tennis. She had a radio in her room, and there were dances in the gym and movies in the auditorium—but that was about it. Still, there was more freedom than there had been when she was living with the doctors, and she was determined to make the best of it.

Although her tennis scholarship paid all of her expenses, she still needed spending money. To earn a few extra bucks, Althea got a job as assistant to the women's physical education director. She earned $40 per month, although she found there wasn't much for her to spend her money on.

Big Woman on Campus

During her second semester at Florida A&M, in the winter of 1950, Althea played in her second Eastern Indoor Championships, which was again held in New York. She won the tournament. The following weekend she played in the National Indoor Championships and made it to the finals before losing 6-2, 6-0 to Nancy Chaffee. Although she was disappointed at her loss, getting to the finals was better than she had expected.

Her success was big news back at Florida A&M. Althea was quickly becoming a campus celebrity. When she returned from her tennis outing there was a crowd of Florida A&M students waiting to greet her at the train station. A band played. The school president gave a speech.

Despite her success, the USLTA still did its best to ignore her. It had been almost three years since Jackie Robinson had integrated Major League Baseball, but the country club set was still unwilling to allow a black woman to play tennis on their courts.

Whereas baseball had been a game for the common person, tennis had always been a sport regarded as not just for white people but just for *rich* white people.

Still, Althea's success had not gone completely unnoticed. One group aware of Althea was the press. Newspapers began to criticize the USLTA for not allowing Althea to play.

Also on Althea's side were white female tennis players. They had played against Althea in indoor tournaments and knew how good she was. They knew that excluding her because she was black was wrong.

Marble Takes a Stand

What was needed was a powerful member of the tennis establishment to take Althea's side and to take it loudly. That person turned out to be Alice Marble, the same former champion who had come to the Cosmopolitan Club to play an exhibition match when Althea was still a teenager. Alice was one of the all-time greatest women tennis players. She had dominated women's tennis during the 1930s.

Marble wrote an article for an issue of *American Lawn Tennis*, the USLTA's official magazine. She wrote: "If tennis is a game for ladies and gentlemen, it's also time we acted more like gentle people . . . If there is anything left in the name of sportsmanship, it's more than time to display what it means to us. If Althea Gibson represents a challenge to the present crop of women players, it's only fair that they should meet that challenge on the courts, where tennis is played. I know those girls, and I can't think of one who would refuse to meet Miss Gibson in competition. She might be soundly beaten for awhile—but she has a much better chance on the courts than in the inner sanctum of the committee, where a different kind of game is being played."

Althea later said that Marble had taken her stand because "of my talent not my color."

The editorial had a dramatic effect on the tennis establishment. Suddenly tournaments that hadn't allowed Althea to play were now accepting her application. She even received invitations to play in tournaments, held at country clubs that had previously been all white.

Althea's first country club match was at the Orange Lawn Tennis Club in South Orange, New Jersey, where she played in the Eastern Grass Court Championships.

Tennis champion Alice Marble (pictured here with Althea) took a stand for Althea, saying that Althea's talent, not her race, should enable her to play in any tournament. (AFP/Getty Images)

Althea won her first match before losing in the second round and being eliminated from the competition.

The next week she integrated her second outdoor tournament by playing in the National Clay Courts Championships in Chicago, Illinois. (Tennis played on clay was a bit slower than tennis played on grass. Different skills were important. Whereas the strongest player often won on grass, the player who hit the ball most accurately often won on clay.) This time she won two matches before losing in the third round.

Then, just a few days before her 23rd birthday, Althea received great news. She had been invited to play in the U.S. National Championships at Forest Hills.

3

FROM FOREST HILLS TO WIMBLEDON

Althea first played in America's biggest tennis tournament at Forest Hills in 1950. The women Althea would be playing against took taxis or limousines to the West Side Country Club tennis facility in Queens. Althea was not quite that fancy. She took the subway to her matches, carrying nothing but two wooden tennis rackets and her gym bag.

Jackie Robinson had carried the weight of all African Americans on his shoulders when he made his debut with the Brooklyn Dodgers three years before. He had broken baseball's color line. Just like Robinson, 23-year-old Althea Gibson had far more pressure on her than was on her white opponents.

First Match

Althea's first match at Forest Hills was on court #14. Tournament officials had scheduled her as far from the clubhouse as possible without playing in someone's backyard. On the main court, movie star Ginger Rogers played an exhibition match, designed to keep fans and the press away from Althea.

The press found her, however. Every time Althea turned around, a photographer took her picture.

Later, Althea recalled, "The whole thing awed me. All this attention, all these people wanting to talk to me and wanting me to say things, patting me on the back and telling me they knew I could do it . . . I couldn't help wishing they would all go away and leave me alone."

Before her match Althea had a brief conversation with Alice Marble, the star who had publicly stood up for her.

"Have courage. Remember, you're just like the rest of us," Alice said.

Althea's opponent that day was Barbara Knapp, of England. Althea defeated her in straight sets: 6-2, 6-2.

Lightning Strikes

After easily winning her first-round match, Althea's first real test in the U.S. National Tennis Championships came in the second round a few days later when she faced Louise Brough, who had won the Forest Hills tournament in 1947 and was a three-time winner at Wimbledon.

Althea practices for her first match at Forest Hills. (Corbis)

This time, because Brough was such a successful tennis player, the organizers of the tournament could not get away with scheduling the match on court 14. The Brough vs. Gibson match on that gray September afternoon took place on Forest Hills' main court, in front of a huge crowd. Sportswriters from all over the country were there. The crowd was sprinkled with familiar show-business faces as well.

As Althea prepared to take the court, her heart was pounding. She was afraid that she would be booed by the white crowd, many of whom believed she shouldn't be competing in a "country club" sport like tennis.

Althea had to perform well. If she didn't, there was no telling how long it would be before another black woman would have a chance to play at that level. In 1947, a black doctor named Reginald Weir had played in a tennis event sanctioned by the white-only USLTA. Dr. Weir had not performed well, causing white fans and tennis officials to exchange "I-told-you-so" glances. Althea wanted her performance to open doors, not help to slam them shut.

Her nerves getting the best of her, Althea lost the first set 6-1. There were hecklers in the crowd. Althea tried to ignore them, but she could not help but hear their taunts.

During the short break between the first and second sets, Althea felt her determination overcome her tension. When the second set began, she played much better.

Stronger than most women tennis players of the time, Althea hit the ball harder, and her power advantage began to show. She won the second set 6-3. The third set would decide the match.

As the third set began, the skies further darkened. In the days before tiebreakers, a set would continue until one player had a two-game lead. After 12 games, the players were tied at six apiece. Serving, Althea won the thirteenth game. By this time, flashes of lightning could be seen in the sky.

Now it was Brough's turn to serve, and the champion was obviously tired. Althea, on the other hand, needing only one more game to win the match, was bouncing on her toes and appeared to be on fresh legs.

Then it started to rain.

Lightning struck a concrete eagle at the top of the stands and sent it toppling downward. Rain came down in sheets. Before the ground crew could put a tarp over it, the grass court was filled with puddles of standing water. No more tennis would be played that day. The match would have to be resumed the next day, weather permitting.

Althea later said, "The delay was the worst thing that could have happened to me." With the rest of the day and night to think about the match, her nerves returned.

On the other side of the net, Brough was given a chance to rest her weary legs.

When the match resumed the next day, once again in front of a huge crowd, Althea found that her momentum was gone. Brough quickly won the third set's 14th game to tie the score at 7-7.

The key to the match came in game 15. With Brough serving, 18 points had to be played before one of the players had a two-point advantage to win the game. Brough held her serve to take an 8-7 lead. Brough then broke Althea's serve to win the set and the match. The pair had played for only 11 minutes on the second day.

Althea rode the subway home, thinking she had blown it.

But just the opposite occurred. She had given the champion such a tough match that she had opened the doors for African Americans. Never again would racists be able to say that African Americans weren't good enough tennis players to compete at the top level.

Now Althea was recognized as one of the best American women tennis players. That much she had anticipated. But she was now also recognized as something else. She was the woman who had integrated tennis. Althea was a hero.

Wimbledon

After her first tournament at Forest Hills, Althea returned to school at Florida A&M. Now that she had integrated women's tennis in the North, the Good Neighbor Tournament in Miami, Florida, decided she should integrate women's tennis in the South as well. They invited her to play in what had previously been an all-white event.

As she played, she could feel the eyes of the spectators on her. "I felt as though I were on display," she said, "being studied through a microscope."

In 1951, Althea's ATA sponsors and USLTA supporters wanted Althea to become the first black woman to play in England's most important tennis tournament, the All-England Tennis Championship. The tournament was most commonly called Wimbledon after the London suburb where it was held. The Wimbledon tournament had been held every year since 1877 and had always been a white-only affair.

Wimbledon was, in many ways, the birthplace of tennis. It was there that many of the rules and regulations of the game had first been written and standardized. The size of the court, height of the net, and method of scorekeeping were all devised at Wimbledon.

In a sense, Wimbledon was the world championship of tennis. Most national championships featured mostly players from that country. But each year the best players from all over the world came to Wimbledon.

The annual tournament was very popular everywhere. But it was most popular in England, where the reigning monarch of England—either a king or a queen—always attended the final matches held at "Centre Court."

Wimbledon would be the biggest tournament of Althea's life. She wanted to make sure that she gave her best possible performance. Althea went to Hamtramck, Michigan (just outside of Detroit), for a few weeks to take lessons from Jean Hoxie, the woman considered by many to be the world's greatest tennis instructor.

Detroit had a large and influential black community. That fact would become better known to the world 10 years later with the success of the Detroit record label called Motown. In 1951, Detroit was known as the home of the most famous black athlete of all, long-time world heavyweight boxing champion Joe Louis.

Althea flew to Detroit. When she arrived at the Detroit airport, she was thrilled to find that Joe had sent a car to pick her up. The boxer had arranged for her to use his private hotel suite during her stay. Her biggest thrill, however, came when she met Joe. He told her that he had purchased a round-trip plane ticket for her to fly across the Atlantic Ocean to London. Althea had been worried about paying for her own travel expenses to Wimbledon. Now she knew that it had been taken care of for her.

A group of Detroit show-business people put on an "Althea Gibson Benefit Show." The show raised $770 to pay for her hotels, meals, and shopping while in England.

Althea was filled with joy and good will as she flew to England. Unfortunately, none of that good feeling went with her onto the tennis court. She won her first two matches and ended forever Wimbledon's days as a white-only club. But in the third round, the quarterfinals, Althea was soundly defeated.

"Unfortunately, a pocketful of money wasn't enough to win for me at Wimbledon. All I got was more experience. Then it was back to another disappointing season in the United States, and a pattern had been set that was to last a long time. I didn't advance in the game as fast as I had hoped I would, and certainly not as fast as a lot of people thought I should," Althea recalled.

Those years were not without their highlights. From 1951 through 1955, Althea won five consecutive ATA championships. She was the country's number-one African-American tennis player. There could be no doubt about that. But when Althea played in USLTA tournaments against white women, she usually won a match or two before she was eliminated by the tougher competition.

She wasn't just the best black woman tennis player in America, either. Althea had established herself as the best black woman tennis player in the world, but she was not satisfied. In 1952, she was ranked the ninth-best American woman tennis player. She had cracked the top 10. But that wasn't good enough. She wasn't going to be satisfied until she was the best woman tennis player in the world.

"The Biggest Disappointment in Tennis"

In 1953, Althea graduated from Florida A&M. Now that her schooling was over, she had to worry about more than just tennis. She had to think about making a living.

The tennis world of the 1950s was very different from that of today. Today, the world's top tennis players are millionaires, winning tens or hundreds of thousands of dollars a week in tennis tournaments. But back then, the great majority of the world's top tennis players were amateurs. Tennis players often came from families that had a lot of money—but that certainly was not true of Althea.

After graduation, Althea got a job as a physical education teacher at Lincoln University, a black college in the strictly segregated community of Jefferson City, Missouri. Althea quickly discovered that there was almost nothing she could do off campus. All of the restaurants refused to serve black people. Even the bowling alley was for whites only. Besides, her salary was only $2,800 per year, which was barely enough to get by.

With this to worry about, her tennis game did not improve much. She did push up to seven in the United States rankings in 1953. But in her first full year out of school, 1954, she dropped to 13. She returned to Forest Hills for the U.S. Championships but lost in the opening round. It was a bitter disappointment.

Althea was disappointed in herself. And the black community, apparently, was disappointed in her as well. *Jet* magazine printed an article about Althea during 1954 entitled "The Biggest Disappointment in Tennis."

Changes

Althea knew something had to be done about her tennis game. She felt like an old car that wasn't running as well as it once had. Both physically and mentally she needed a complete overhaul.

During her slump she often stayed for long stretches with her friend Rosemary Darben in the Darben family's New Jersey home. During these visits Rosemary's brother Will and Althea soon became very good friends. In 1953 Will proposed marriage to Althea. She turned him down because, although she felt very close to him, she was not in love with him.

It was during 1954, as she suffered through her tennis slump, that Althea met part-time cab driver and part-time tennis instructor Sydney Llewellyn. He had been born and raised in Jamaica in the West Indies.

Sydney and Althea hit it off and he agreed to tune up her tennis game. He told her to forget everything she knew. They started with the fundamentals and worked from there. She changed the way she gripped the tennis racket. She changed the way she swung it. She changed the way she went about battling an opponent. At 5'11 and well muscled, Althea was stronger and had longer legs than her opponents. Sydney taught her to use these advantages. Soon everything changed for Althea—this time for the better.

Sydney knew that Althea's problem had little to do with how she gripped or swung the racket. Her problem had to do with her mind. There was something in her that told her that she couldn't be the best. There was something that kept her from playing the way she should (and could). When playing the best tennis players in the world, Althea let the pressure get to her. By taking her game apart and putting it back together again, Sydney tried to give Althea something she had always lacked: real confidence.

Althea was not a kid anymore. She was 26 in 1954. If she was going to make a move to become the world's greatest woman tennis player, she was going to have to do it soon. Female athletes reached their prime quicker than men. As athletes, women aged more quickly.

While Sydney Llewellyn was changing Althea's tennis game, her personal life was changing as well. Quite unexpectedly, Althea fell in love with another teacher at Lincoln University. He was the Reserve Officers' Training Corps (ROTC) instructor, who trained college students to be army officers. He was an army captain, and during their short but intense romance, he advised Althea to join the army.

Joining the army, the captain said, was the answer to her financial problems. She had a college degree and so could join the Women's Army Corps as an officer. She could retire after 20 years and receive a pension check for the rest of her life. Of course, it would mean an end to Althea's tennis career, but Althea figured that wasn't so bad. If she was going to be a tennis champion, it would have happened by now.

So Althea planned to play at Forest Hills one more time in 1955 and then say goodbye to tennis and join the army. At the U.S. Championships at Forest Hills, she gave a typical performance, losing in the third round.

4

GOODWILL TOUR

Although Althea's 1955 performance at Forest Hills was disappointing, while there she was approached by Renville McMann, the club president. He told her that there was going to be a goodwill tour of Southeast Asia for the U.S. State Department. Two men and two women tennis players would go on the trip. He told her the State Department wanted Althea to be one of the women. Althea did not have to think long before making her decision.

"It would be an honor," she told McMann.

Thus, Althea forgot about joining the army and agreed to go on the goodwill tour. She had been craving something interesting to do, and this fit the bill perfectly. Her anticipation grew even further when she learned that she would be traveling with Karol Fageros, Ham Richardson, and Bob Perry, all players she knew and liked.

As for Karol, Althea wrote, "I couldn't think of anybody I would rather spend a couple of months with."

The trip took Althea to exotic places beyond her imagination. She visited Malaysia, Pakistan, Indonesia, India, Ceylon, Burma, and Thailand.

"We had some great adventures," she later recalled. She remembered being entertained by belly dancers, eating strange foods, and visiting places in Pakistan where women were not supposed to be seen in public.

Because the lands she visited were populated by dark-skinned people, Althea quickly found that she was the "star" of the tour. "The kids looked at me as I played with awe and amazement," she later recalled.

As the only African American among white people, Althea was lonely throughout many of her tennis experiences. But on the goodwill tour, Althea grew closer to her three tourmates than she had to any other white people ever (closer, in fact, than she had been to just about anyone in her life).

Maybe it was the friendship she was feeling or the sense of adventure, but during her tour of Asia, Althea's tennis got much better. She felt the improvements during the many exhibition matches she played while on tour. She then proved that her progress was real by winning the All-Asian Tennis Tournament in Burma.

Althea was very sad when the tour ended. She later called the tour the most completely satisfying and rewarding thing she had ever done. She couldn't believe that, only a few weeks before, she had been considering giving up her career as a tennis player to join the army.

Now Althea's tennis game was once again the most important thing in her life. She concentrated on her game harder than ever.

The 1956 French Championships

While the other tennis players on the goodwill tour returned immediately to the United States, Althea stayed in Europe to play tennis against international competition. Beginning with her victory in Burma, Althea played in 18 international tournaments and won sixteen of them. This included a victory in the 1956 French Championships, which—along with Wimbledon, Forest Hills, and the Australian Championships—was one of the most important tennis tournaments in the world. The thing that made the French Championships different from other tournaments was that it was played on clay courts.

The tournament's most famous moment came on the tennis court, but it didn't have much to do with tennis. Althea was playing Angela Buxton in the semifinals when she felt a bra-strap break. Angela and Althea met at the net. They decided that Althea had better retreat to the dressing room to change her clothes. Althea did this very quickly, thinking about the crowd she was making wait.

When Althea returned to the court, she found a meeting of tournament officials going on. Althea, it turned out, had left the court without permission. She could have been disqualified from the tournament if Angela asked them to do it. Angela explained that having Althea disqualified because her bra broke was the last thing she wanted to do. She wanted to win or lose the match on the court. So the officials left, the match continued, and Althea won. That put her into the finals against another Angela: Angela Mortimer.

That match between Gibson and Buxton will probably always be remembered as the "bra-strap match." But it was historic for another reason. Angela Buxton was of the Jewish faith. Like Althea, she had been forced to break down a few social barriers of her own.

Althea and Angela had first played in India and had gotten along, even though they were very different. Angela was the granddaughter of Russian Jews. She grew up in England, a member of a wealthy family.

But Althea and Angela had something in common, something that set them apart from all of the other top-women tennis players. They had both had to battle against prejudice to get where they were. Being very good at tennis wasn't enough. They had to deal with the people who thought they didn't belong, regardless of their talent, because of their race or religion.

For those who were working for equal opportunities for everyone, it must have been satisfying to see a Jewish woman playing an African American in the French Championships.

Althea won the French Championships (the same tournament today known as the French Open) on May 20, 1956, with a 6-3, 11-9 victory over England's Angela Mortimer. Althea had become the first black woman to win one of the world's major tennis tournaments.

Getting "Overtennised"

Because Althea had been playing so well lately, she was no longer the underdog. With Wimbledon approaching, Althea was the favorite to win.

But Althea had played too much tennis in too short a time. She later referred to her state as "overtennised." In other words, she was tired.

She was also saddened to find that the attitude of the British tennis-going public toward black tennis players had not changed much. After playing before wildly cheering crowds all over Asia and in France, English crowds clenched their teeth and offered only "polite" applause. Althea, for the first time in what seemed like a long while, could feel racial hatred in the crowd.

On the night before her quarterfinals match against Shirley Fry, Althea told a reporter with the *London Daily Mail*: "After ten years of tennis, I am still a poor Negress, as poor as when I was picked off the back streets of Harlem and given the chance to work myself up to stardom. I have traveled to many countries—in Europe, Asia, and Africa—in comfort. I have stayed in the best hotels, and met many rich people. I am much richer in knowledge and experience. But I have no money. I have no apartment or even a room of my own anywhere in America. I have no clothes beyond those with which I travel around. And I like clothes. Unfortunately, I have no gift for making them, and I can't afford many of the wide variety of cheap, ready-to-wear American dresses which other American girls buy . . . I haven't been able to help my mother and my father, and the rest of my family. They are still poor, very poor . . ."

The next day, Althea lost in the quarterfinals at Wimbledon (4-6, 6-3, 6-4) to another American, Shirley Fry.

A reporter at court side wrote this of the match: "Today, nerves, influenced by a packed center court, and perhaps even by the presence in the royal box of the Duchess of Kent, played a great part in the match. The nerves of Miss Fry, who had played so many a struggle on Wimbledon's main court, were the more firm."

About the racism everyone had felt in the crowd, Scottie Hall of the *London Sunday Graphic* newspaper wrote,

"You know the wonderful feeling you get in a theater when an audience rises to the first entrance of a well-loved star? I wish it had been like that. But it wasn't. It was an unspoken, unexpressed but felt anti-Gibson atmosphere." The feeling, he explained, was "eerie." The crowd worried that if Althea won at Wimbledon, the sport would be overrun by black women, just as boxing had been populated by many boxers of African heritage after Joe Louis became the world heavyweight champion.

First Wimbledon Title

Both Althea, because she was black, and Angela Buxton, because she was Jewish, had trouble finding doubles partners in 1956. So they decided to team up together.

The team-up turned out to be magical. When Angela would have a short slump, Althea would do something amazing to make up for it. When Althea found herself briefly tired and moving a little slow, Angela would have a burst of energy. That kept their opponents from taking advantage.

Ultimately, Althea and Angela won the Wimbledon doubles tournament. It was Althea's first major title, but it was not a single's title, which is what Althea so desired. Althea's disappointment was evident in her autobiography, which she wrote a few years later. In it she never once mentions that she and Angela Buxton were the 1956 Wimbledon ladies' doubles champions.

After Wimbledon, Althea returned to the United States, where she played in the National Clay Courts Championships in Chicago. In Chicago, Althea again lost to Shirley Fry, who was quickly becoming Althea's number-one rival for best woman tennis player in the world.

Althea won a couple of minor tournaments to prepare herself for the 1956 Forest Hills tournament. For the first time she made it all the way to the finals. But again she lost to Shirley Fry: 6-3, 6-4.

"Would you like to come back next year?" a reporter asked Althea after her loss.

"If I'm asked," she replied. She was disappointed and mad at herself but determined to try again.

Making Career Strides

Despite her loss in the finals at Forest Hills, Althea had one of the greatest years ever for a woman tennis player. She rose to number two in the world rankings. Only two years before, she had been ranked thirteenth. *World Tennis Magazine* called it "one of the fastest climbs to the top" in women's tennis history. No one was disappointed in Althea any longer.

The days of tennis tournament organizers looking the other way when making out the invitations were over. Tennis fans around the world wanted to see Althea play. And so, by invitation, in 1956 she also played a series of tournaments in Australia. Also making the trip was her archrival, the world's number-one women's player: Shirley Fry. In the four tournaments they played, each won two. Fry won the Victorian and Australian tournaments, while Althea came out on top in the New South Wales and South Australian tournaments.

Gibson and Fry might have been rivals on the court, but off the court they became very good friends. In Australia they spent a great deal of time together, touring the country. Although this tour was in no way sponsored by the U.S. government, Althea felt as if her role as a goodwill ambassador never ended. She loved meeting the people, and the Australians loved her.

In Australia, while playing in the city of Sydney, Shirley Fry fell in love with an American there and decided to marry him. When Althea left Australia to defend her Asian Championship in Colombo, Ceylon, Fry stayed behind, planning her wedding.

In Colombo, Althea became the two-time Asian women's champion by defeating Pat Ward of England in the finals. Althea then returned to the United States and took it easy. She wanted to be well rested for the 1957 tennis season.

In 1956 Althea had made the mistake of playing in all three warm-up tournaments in England, before Wimbledon. She had ended up playing in the big tournament exhausted and had run out of gas. She was not going to make that mistake again. She went to Chicago and won the National Clay Courts Tournament. After that she led a U.S. team to victory over Great Britain in the Wightman Cup competition.

But she didn't wear herself out in England playing several tournaments before Wimbledon. This year, she saved her energy for "The Big One."

It was around this time that Althea took up a new sport: golf. Playing golf on public courses during her down time helped her relax. Not only was it a lot of fun, but Althea quickly realized that she was very good at it.

Her swing, her putting, and her ability to judge distances and to use her imagination when she was in trouble made her an outstanding golfer. Club pros told her that with a year or two of work she could play pro golf. Althea took that idea and put it on a back burner.

Strong and Confident

Althea arrived in Wimbledon in 1957 feeling great. She felt as strong and confident as ever. The tournament did not get off to the greatest start, however. She was scheduled to play

Suzy Kormoczy in the opening round. Suzy was a Hungarian who always gave Althea a tough match. It was no different on this occasion. Suzy made Althea work for every point. The match was long and grueling, more so than the score showed. Althea won the match 6-4, 6-4—but the Hungarian had made sure that, when it was over, Althea knew she had been challenged.

Things went easier for Althea's next couple of matches. In the semifinals Althea was pitted against one of England's favorites, Christine Truman. The British teenager was the one every British tennis fan wanted to see win the tournament, so when Althea took the court that day, she once again found herself in the role of the villain.

There was a time when the tight-lipped crowd might have made Althea feel so uncomfortable that she would not have been able to play her best. Those days were over. Despite the fact that the crowd was clearly rooting for her opponent, Althea attacked hard and played flawless tennis. In fact, Althea played some of the best tennis any woman had ever played. She won 6-1, 6-1.

When the match was over, a funny thing happened. Although the crowd had started out against her, they had been so dazzled by the quality of Althea's play that they gave her a standing ovation.

And so, with that stunning performance, Althea earned her first chance to play in the finals at Wimbledon. The

Althea on the courts at Wimbledon, 1957 (Corbis)

match, as it was every year, was held on the center court and in the audience was England's Queen Elizabeth II.

The night before the match Althea showed signs of being nervous. Luckily, a couple of her best friends from America were there to keep her company and help her stay calm. At Wimbledon, the custom was for each woman tennis player to curtsy for the queen before the match started. Having never curtsied before, Althea spent much of the night before the finals practicing. The next day, when the time came, her curtsy for the queen was flawless. As far as Althea was concerned, the tough part was over. Now all she had to do was play great tennis—and she did.

"At Last!"

The final match was a battle between Americans—East Coast versus West Coast. Althea's opponent was Darlene Hard from California. Althea took charge in the match right away. The first set lasted a short 25 minutes, with Althea finishing on top, 6-3.

One set away from a Wimbledon championship, Althea's game became nothing short of brilliant. The second set went just as smoothly as the first. Well before it was over, Darlene was hanging her head. She sensed that it was not her day. Althea served harder and ran faster than she ever had before. The match was over in less than an hour.

Althea screamed, "At last!" and ran to the net to shake hands with her thoroughly defeated opponent. Then, her knees shaking slightly, she watched as a red carpet was rolled out. The queen left her royal box and approached Althea to present her with her trophy. She curtsied again. This time it was easy. She shook hands with the queen, who congratulated her. Althea beamed with pride. All of her life she had wanted to be somebody. Now there was no doubt in her mind that she was.

Years later, Howard University Sports Information Director Edward Hill recalled how much pride Althea's victory gave the black community. "Up until that point heroes like Jackie Robinson, Willie Mays, and Jim Brown had all given great pride to people of color. On the female side there were very few heroes so this made Althea's accomplishments all the more amazing," Hill said.

When Althea got back to her hotel in Paris she found telegrams waiting for her from the President of the United States, Dwight Eisenhower, the Governor of New York State, Averill Harriman, and her old friend from her Harlem days, boxing champion Sugar Ray Robinson.

The telegram from the president read:

Dear Miss Gibson:

Many Americans, including myself, have watched with increasing admiration your sustained and successful effort to win the heights in the tennis world. Millions of your fellow citizens would, if they could, join with me in felicitations on your outstanding victory at Wimbledon.

Recognizing the odds you faced, we have applauded your courage, persistence and application.

Certainly it is not easy for anyone to stand in the center court at Wimbledon and, in the glare of world publicity and under the critical gaze of thousands of spectators, do his or her very best. You met the challenge superbly.

With best wishes,
Dwight D. Eisenhower

As she read the telegram she thought about just how far from 143rd Street she was. That night she got to put on her fanciest dress and attend the Wimbledon Ball, where she was crowned "Queen of the Ball." She gave a speech.

"In the words of your distinguished Mr. Churchill," Althea said, referring to Great Britain's then-Prime Minister, "this is my finest hour. This is the hour I will remember always as the crowning conclusion to a long and wonderful journey. It all started in one of New York's play streets when Buddy Walker, a play-street supervisor, reached beyond his grasp of a handful of youngsters playing paddle tennis. He said, 'Althea, I believe you could become a good lawn tennis player,' and with those words he handed me my first tennis racket and started me hitting against a handball court. Tonight, I thank Buddy Walker for a most satisfying victory. But the victory is not mine alone. It belongs to many people who play an important part in the picture here tonight. To mention them all would take too long, but I cannot help but recall a few whose encouragement and faith permit my presence here tonight."

She went on to thank Drs. Robert W. Johnson and Hubert A. Eaton, who had allowed her to live in their homes and whose assistance had permitted her to complete high school. She thanked her current coach Sydney Llewellyn, the ATA, and the USLTA.

"And how could I forget my good friend and former partner, Angela Buxton, whose friendship I shall always cherish," Althea said. She thanked her competitors and the tennis fans of England. She then concluded: "Your Highness, my friends, I am humbly grateful and deeply aware of the responsibility involved in the wearing of this crown. God grant that I may wear it with dignity, defend it with honor, and, when my day is done, relinquish it graciously. I thank you."

Then, while everyone—including members of the royal family—gathered around to watch, she danced with the winner of the male competition, Lew Hoad. Following her magical day, Althea had an equally magical night.

Celebrations

Althea returned to the United States, where there was more celebrating. A large crowd gathered to meet her

Althea was given a tickertape parade in New York after her victory at Wimbledon in 1957. (Corbis)

plane at the airport. Among those gathered were newspaper reporters, politicians, and Althea's mother. Then it was up to Harlem, where the streets were lined with many people cheering Althea.

Regarding her successful homecoming, Althea later wrote about how thrilled she was to see "all those people" so happy that "one of the neighbors' children had gone out into the world and done something big."

The following day she received a ticker-tape parade along Broadway in Manhattan. She rode in a car and waved to her thousands of gathered fans. People tossed pieces of paper out of windows from the tall buildings on either side of the street. At the end of the parade Mayor Robert Wagner presented Althea with a gold medallion. Then she headed uptown to the luxurious Waldorf-Astoria Hotel where there was a gala luncheon held in her honor.

In 1957, Althea won the Babe Didrikson Zaharias Trophy as America's outstanding female athlete—not just in tennis but in any sport. Because of her fame, invitations were coming in from all around the world for Althea to play. She decided to take advantage. By accepting invitations to play in tournaments on islands in the Caribbean Sea and in South America (all expenses paid by the tournament's promoters, of course) she got to see those places for free.

5

AMERICA'S OUTSTANDING FEMALE ATHLETE

Althea suddenly found herself to be a very important African-American figure. She was a groundbreaker, and many people were interested in what she had to say about civil rights.

Although Althea had the utmost respect for African-American civil rights leaders, such as Dr. Martin Luther King Jr., she had no urge to become such a leader. She felt she was not skilled at giving speeches, and she was content to allow others, who she felt were better qualified, to make speeches about the plight of black people in the United States and around the world.

There were editorials written in the black press that maybe Althea wasn't doing enough to advance black causes, considering her role as a leading black athlete. To those criticisms, Althea replied, "I feel strongly that I can do more good my way than I could by militant crusading. I want my success to speak for itself as an advertisement for my race."

In other words, Althea felt that because she had won major tennis tournaments all over the world, this was proof that black women belonged in these tournaments. No speeches were necessary. All she wanted to do was play tennis.

Althea's self-esteem was at an all-time high. As she said at the time, "My pleasures and interests are simple. I have no lofty, overpowering ambition. All I want is to be able to play tennis, sing, sleep peacefully, have three square meals a day, a regular income, and no worries. I don't feel any need to be a King Midas with a whole string of people hanging on me to be supported. I don't want to be put on a pedestal. I just want to be reasonably successful and live a normal life with all of the conveniences to make it so."

Althea had found her identity. She was a tennis champion, and she was playing the best tennis of her life. Her hot streak continued throughout 1957 and into 1958.

Back to Forest Hills

In 1957 Althea again headed to the U.S. Championship in Forest Hills, the last big event of the year. In the opening round Althea defeated Karol Fageros, who had accompanied Althea on the Asian goodwill tour. Althea won in straight sets by the close scores of 6-4, 6-4.

Althea won her next four matches as well, and she still had yet to lose a set in the tournament. Althea's opponent in the finals was Louise Brough, the same woman who had defeated Althea the first time she ever played at Forest Hills, when the lightning bolt struck the grandstand.

The two were very different tennis players than when they had first competed. Althea had gotten better. Louise had not. On this day Althea had no trouble defeating Louise. She won 6-3, 6-2, for her second consecutive Forest Hills victory.

Her trophy was given to her by Richard Nixon, who was at that time vice president of the United States. The crowd, which only a few years before had been tight-lipped and grim as they watched Althea play, now rose to their feet and gave her a standing ovation.

The 1958 season started with the Wightman Cup competition, once again between the United States and Great Britain. Things did not go as well this year, however, for the Americans. Althea and the rest of the U.S. team played poorly and Great Britain took the cup.

That same year Althea was approached by a literary agent, who asked Althea to begin working on her autobiography. That book, *I Always Wanted to Be Somebody,* was released in 1958.

Defending Her Wimbledon Title

Next up in 1958 was Wimbledon. When Althea arrived at Wimbledon for the 1958 tournament, she knew that she had to win again, just to force people to believe that her first win there had been real. According to Althea: "In sports, you simply aren't considered a real champion until you have defended your title successfully. Winning it once can be a fluke; winning it twice proves you are the best."

In her quarterfinal match on the English grass courts, Althea had to face England's best female tennis player, Shirley Bloomer, who gave Althea a tough match. Gibson and Bloomer split the first two sets, but Althea managed to finish on top in the third set to move in.

Althea's semifinal match was much easier. She took only a little more than a half-hour to eliminate Ann Haydon. In the 14 games played in the match, Althea won all but two of them.

That put Althea in the finals, pitted this time against Angela Mortimer. She defeated Mortimer in straight sets,

Althea holds the trophy for her second victory at the Wimbledon Women's Singles tournament. (Getty Images)

8-6, 6-2, and for the second year in a row she won Wimbledon. She curtseyed for the queen and, that night, was the star of the ball in her beautiful formal gown. (It would be more than 30 years before another black woman, Zina Garrison in 1990, would reach the finals at Wimbledon. Venus Williams won at Wimbledon in 2000. In 1975, Arthur Ashe became the first black man to win at Wimbledon.)

As it turned out, that was the last time Althea would ever compete at Wimbledon. At the time, tennis tournaments were strictly divided between amateur and professional contests. Today, all top tennis players are professional, and the prize money for top players can turn them quickly into millionaires. And there are few tennis tournaments left in the world in which professionals are not allowed to compete. Today, professional athletes are even allowed to compete for their country in the Olympics.

But that was not the case in 1958. An athlete who accepted money for playing her sport would have been stripped of her amateur status and thus would not have been allowed to play in amateur tournaments anymore. Althea played 17 matches at Wimbledon, and she won 16 of them. She played in three singles tournaments. Twice she came away the champion. But in stark contrast to today's tennis champions, she never received money for playing, thereby retaining her amateur status.

Defending Her National Championship

After playing in, and winning, a couple of warm-up tournaments, Althea returned to Forest Hills at the end of the 1958 season to defend her national title. Althea destroyed the competition. She won every set until she reached the finals. In that match she again faced California-girl Darlene Hard. During their first set Althea appeared to be, for the first time in a long time, the second-best tennis player. Hard won the first set 6-3.

After taking a licking in the first set, something woke up inside Althea. She began to play great. Hard no longer looked like the best player on the court. Althea cruised through the next two sets, winning 6-1 and 6-2. Althea was once again the U.S. champion.

In 1958, as she had the previous year, Althea won the Babe Didrikson Zaharias Woman Athlete of the Year trophy. She was at the top of the world of women's tennis. There was no place to go but down—unless she found a different world in which to compete.

Making a Living

Soon after winning the Zaharias trophy, Althea announced that she was retiring as an amateur tennis player. She also announced that she was "retiring" from all tennis playing for at least a year. She told the press that her reason for ending her amateur career was easy.

She needed to make money. She had been enriched, she said, in so many ways because of the tennis career that had taken her around the world. But still she was broke.

Althea wanted to play tennis for a living, but she wasn't at all sure that she could make enough playing tennis to support herself. At the time, there were very few professional tournaments, and those consisted of men only.

But she needed to get a job of some sort. She was 31 years old, and her small New York City apartment was furnished with chairs and tables that others had left at the curb. And she needed to do something about her parents, who were still poor and living in a Harlem slum.

If Althea had been a white woman, she would have had her choice of becoming the club pro at any country club in the world. (The club pro gives lessons to club members.) Although this would not have been as much fun as playing competitive tennis for a living, being a club pro paid a very nice salary.

But as a black woman, Althea received no offers at all.

Althea decided to use her star status as a career booster and try to make her money doing something other than playing tennis. Althea was thinking about show business. There was no denying that Althea enjoyed performing in front of crowds. And she was a very good singer. Thus, she decided to try to launch a singing career.

Althea recalled, "The saxophone that Sugar Ray bought me, and the band work I did while I was going to high school in Wilmington, sidetracked my singing interests for a while. But saxophone or no saxophone, I used to grab every chance I got to sing on stage both in high school and college."

She remembered that she had wanted to minor in music at Florida A&M, but her faculty advisers had talked her out of it. They had said that athletics and music don't mix. Now she regretted that she hadn't studied music more.

Shortly before her retirement from tennis, she tried to convince her coach-turned-manager, Sydney Llewellyn, that she could make money with her music. Like her college advisers, he believed that concentrating on a singing career would wreck her tennis game. It took some work, but Althea finally convinced him that this was not so. She could be a tennis player and a singer, too.

If Althea was going to be a singer, Sydney wanted to make sure she would be a successful one. He arranged for her to take singing lessons with Professor James Kennedy, who was the director of speech and voice at Long Island University.

"I began working with him three times a week in his office at the university," Althea remembered. "He was very encouraging and helpful. I began to feel that I might really have a chance of getting somewhere."

In addition to singing, Althea took a crack at acting. Hollywood wanted her in the movies. In 1959, Althea made her acting debut in the movie *The Horse Soldiers*. Because Hollywood in those days only cast African Americans in a small number of roles, Althea was forced to play a maid in the movie. In the movie her lines mostly consisted of stereotyped phrases such as "yassuh" and "yassim."

There were also lines in the script that Althea thought were too insulting to black women. She told the director that they could fire her if they wanted to, but she was not going to say those lines in the movie. After many meetings, the lines were cut.

That same year, Althea made her professional singing debut. Her talents had been discovered at a dinner held in the honor of W. C. Handy, the songwriter called the "Father of the Blues." The dinner was held at the Waldorf-Astoria hotel in New York. It was the same hotel in which she had received her gala dinner after her first Wimbledon victory. Althea sang an obscure, untitled song that Handy had written in the 1920s.

"With Professor Kennedy's help, I got by," she later said. But she did better than that. She impressed the audience, which included members of the music industry.

Handy was pleased with Althea's rendition of one of his old songs. Also in the audience was Henry Onorati, the vice president of Dot Records. He asked her to come in and visit his studio to make a demo record, like an audition, and when that went well he invited her to make an album.

Her album was called *Althea Gibson Sings*. The first song on the album was called "So Much to Live For." Althea had a nice voice, but many felt that she was out of her league in the competitive music industry.

She made two television appearances on the popular *Ed Sullivan Show*. The show's producers felt that a tennis star that sang was a novelty act. "I couldn't be sure if the Sullivan show invitation came because I was a good singer, or because I was a good tennis player," Althea later said.

But that was the end of her singing career. Once the novelty wore off, no one wanted to pay to hear Althea sing. However, this was only a minor disappointment as far as Althea was concerned. "I have no burning desire to set the world on fire as a singer," she later said. Overall, she had enjoyed her show-business experience.

Life with the Harlem Globetrotters

In 1960, Althea finally found a steady job. And to her delight it was as a tennis player. She was signed by Abe Saperstein to tour with the Harlem Globetrotters, a group of clownish but talented basketball players who combined slapstick humor with great basketball skills. Their nightly opponents were the Washington Generals. The Generals were a hapless group that, after thousands of shows, was still waiting for their first win.

Saperstein was the manager of the Globetrotters and wanted Althea to play tennis as a warm-up act for the team. They would put a net up and she could play against an opponent right on the basketball court. Sometimes she would play the local star, and sometimes another pro was hired to be Althea's opponent. That role was played most often by Karol Fageros. Karol had been on the Asia goodwill trip. She was a pretty blonde, Althea's friend, and a comfortable traveling partner.

Althea, like the Globetrotters, always won.

Still, life with the Globetrotters was tough. They traveled far more than Althea ever had as a tennis player. In tennis, she had changed cities every week. Since the Globetrotters played one-nighters, they changed cities every day.

Other opportunities to make money with her tennis racket cropped up as well. For the first time there were women's pro tennis tournaments, and Althea won just about all of them. The prize money was nothing like it is today, as tournaments were often local events sponsored by sporting goods stores. But it was still a job, and playing tennis was still fun. In 1960, Althea was the Women's Pro Singles champion.

Althea worked for Althea Gibson Enterprises Inc., the corporation of moneymaking ventures formed by Althea, her coach/manager Sydney, and her lawyer. By the summer of 1960, Althea had enough money to move into a larger apartment, with much better furniture.

She also bought a big house in the suburbs for her mother and father. Althea later wrote about how proud she was to get her parents away from the filth, heat, and danger of the slum and into the green-grass and blue-sky world of the suburbs.

Abe Saperstein asked Althea to come with the Globetrotters on their European Tour, but she turned down the invitation. She had a better idea. Her matches had been very popular at the Globetrotters games, so popular that, she figured, she could tour with her own show. It would be the Althea Gibson Show, and she would be the star, not the warm-up act. She would reverse things. A basketball game would start the show, and then she would come out and play tennis.

Althea put together the troupe and took her act on the road. The trouble was that nobody bought tickets. As it turned out, most of the people at the Globetrotters games were there to see the Globetrotters; they weren't interested in imitation sports shows. And, as it turned out, without the Globetrotters, there weren't that many people who wanted to see Althea play in a spoof of a tennis exhibition.

After three months, the remainder of the tour was canceled. Althea had lost all of her money and then some. She was deeply in debt—and she was tired of playing tennis in front of empty seats. Althea Gibson Enterprises went out of business.

6

A NEW SPORT

To help herself get out of debt, Althea took a well-paying job as the spokesperson for the Ward Baking Company, makers of Tip Top Bread. She appeared in print ads and traveled from city to city making appearances on behalf of Tip Top Bread.

She gave inspirational speeches at these events. She took questions from the audience and gave positive and uplifting responses. She did not have to do any full commercials for Tip Top. As long as she mentioned the brand name of the bread and the name of the bakery a few times during her speech, her bosses were happy. She ended her presentations with a rousing song and usually received a standing ovation. For this she received a $25,000 annual salary, which was very good in 1961.

Audiences viewed Althea as a woman of courage and accomplishment. But, deep inside, Althea was not feeling positive, and she did not find her job uplifting. She felt that her glory days were behind her and that she had nothing to look forward to. At least nothing that could compare with winning at Wimbledon or at Forest Hills.

The best part about her Tip Top tour was that she got to play golf. And, because she traveled so much, she got to play on a wide variety of great courses. The relaxation she felt while playing golf helped her feel better.

The thing that was missing in her life, she realized, was athletic competition. Thinking of the future, she decided not to go back into tennis. Instead she recalled the words of those club pros who had watched her play in the mid-1950s.

"A little work and you could be the best," they would say.

She decided to find out if they were right. She was a gifted athlete. She had already become the best in the world at one sport. She saw no reason why she couldn't become the best in two sports.

Althea officially dropped tennis as her number-one athletic activity. She took up a sport that was kinder to her aging legs: golf.

Days on the Golf Course

One day, as Althea carried her clubs to the first tee for an afternoon round, a newspaper reporter ran up to her.

"Could you say something about your future plans for golf, Miss Gibson?" he asked.

"No particular plans," Althea replied.

"You've been on the links an awful lot lately."

"Oh well. Anybody can come here. It's open to the public," she said.

There was a pause as Althea realized she had not responded to the reporter's satisfaction.

"I just play for fun," she said. "To relax, when I am not at work."

"A couple of years ago, you said you were not interested in returning to pro tennis. Would you say that a golfing career is out of the question for you?"

"Well, anything is possible," she said.

Golf became Althea's obsession. She realized that she would be competing against life-long golfers who grew up with a golf club in their hands. Althea was a newcomer to the sport. She was 33 years old. She had only been playing the game for four years.

Though Althea had a bundle of raw talent, she felt her lack of experience would be her undoing if she played in a tournament against the best lady golfers in the world.

Althea learned how to strike a golf ball with relative ease. The even strain of emotions that golfers need to compete was harder for Althea to learn. In tennis, the anxiety that came from making a mistake could quickly be channeled into strength and speed. But playing golf, Althea had to learn to stay calm even when she wanted to scream with frustration. With time she learned to forget the bad shot and to concentrate on making the next shot a good one.

Her efforts to perfect her golf game were enhanced by a man named Jerry Volpe. He was a professional golfer and the owner of the Englewood Golf Club in New Jersey. Volpe was impressed by Althea's game and gave her an "honorary" membership to his club. She would be the first African American to be allowed to play the Englewood course. With her membership, she could play the Englewood course as much as she wanted for free, without having to pay greens fees at public courses as she had before.

Ready to Turn Pro

By 1962, Althea felt she was ready to play with the pros. That was when she discovered another problem with starting a career as a professional golfer was like a familiar old slap in the face: racial prejudice. Althea realized quickly enough that the lady's pro golf tour was an all-white affair. There were no black women on the tour. There had never been a black woman on the tour. It would be two years before Althea would be able to break that color barrier.

Althea's strategy was simple. It was the same strategy she had used when breaking the color barrier in lady's tennis. She was going to prove to the world that she deserved to be on the women's golf tour. Once she did that, there would be social pressure for her to compete

During the 1960s, Althea tried her hand at professional golf, another sport for which she showed a natural talent.
(Associated Press)

against the best, and the walls in her way would come tumbling down.

This attempt at a new career would not have been possible if it hadn't been for the Tip Top Bread people. They agreed to keep paying Althea to represent the company, even though she had transformed from a tennis player into a golfer. Her schedule was rearranged so that she would be able to play 18 holes every day.

In two years she went from shooting in the low 80s (the number of strokes it takes to complete an 18-hole round) to shooting in the low 70s, where she needed to be to play tournament golf.

Talking to reporters, Althea made it clear that integration was on her mind when it came to golf.

"My hope is that I can bring more Negroes into the game," she said.

As had been true in the tennis world, Althea found little racial objection from her fellow women golfers. Luckily for Althea, the Ladies Professional Golf Association (LPGA) was run by the athletes. It was agreed that, if Althea entered an "open" tournament and qualified to compete, the LPGA would do nothing to stop her from competing.

She had to finish in the top fifth of the entrants during qualifying rounds three weeks in a row to get to play in the tournament. She accomplished this twice in a row on public courses, but the third week's qualification rounds were held at a country club.

At first the country club did not want Althea to play at all but finally compromised with the LPGA. Althea would be able to play on the golf course. But, because she was black, she would not be able to use the clubhouse facilities. She could not go inside. That suited Althea fine. The golf course was the only part of the club she was interested in.

Althea quickly realized that the country club's decision was going to do a lot more to help her cause than to hurt it. The press was outraged by the country club's decision. Editorials appeared calling for equal opportunity for LPGA players.

Althea used that hostile setting to play some of the best golf of her life. She had finished in the top fifth of the field three weeks in a row. That earned Althea her LPGA Player's Card. She was now a member of the tour.

The LPGA was strongly behind Althea. On several occasions during the summer of 1964, the LPGA refused to play their tournament at a country club because the club wouldn't let one of their players in the clubhouse. The tournament was moved to a new club, where Althea was treated more politely.

Despite her social successes, Althea's first few years as a pro golfer were wildly inconsistent. She would be great one day and not so great the next. If things kept up like that, she was not going to be able to make a living as a golfer. In 1964 her golf winnings totaled $560. The top moneymaker on the tour earned $29,800.

That year, she was still a spokesperson for the Ward Baking Company, so she made money that way. But in 1965 Althea put in more time trying to be a successful pro golfer than she did making appearances for Tip Top Bread. The bread company let her go, because she could no longer put enough time into promoting their product.

Without a sponsor, Althea had to pay her own travel bills. To do this, she took out a loan at the bank. That year she made $1,595 playing golf, nowhere near enough to pay back the loan.

Will Darben

As Althea was making the transition from tennis player to golfer, an old friend had re-entered her life. It was Will Darben, brother of her good friend Rosemary Darben. She had spent long stretches living at the Darben home when she was in the middle of her early-1950s slump.

Will had fallen in love with her and had proposed. She turned him down. Now he was back and he became her constant companion as she grew more comfortable on the golf course.

In 1965, 12 years after his first proposal, Will once again asked Althea to marry him and this time she said yes. Althea married Will Darben in Las Vegas, Nevada.

The newly married couple was very happy. Althea had always known that Will played the piano, but after they were married she was pleased to learn that he wrote songs as well. Darben took care of Althea's money woes and agreed to finance her pro golf career. In 1966, Althea played some of her best golf. Although Will rarely got to see Althea play because his job kept him from traveling, her game was better than ever. She broke one course record with a 68. She made more than $3,000 that year. It still wasn't very much money, but each year Althea was making much more than she had the year before.

During one 1967 interview, Althea again let it be known that she was proud of her civil rights efforts. "If my being here and playing golf can be of some stimulation to other young ladies of my race to play golf, then I feel I've made a contribution," she said.

Althea's success on the golf course, unfortunately, peaked in 1967. She continued to play golf for a living for another three years, but her game did not improve. In fact, it slipped.

Back to Tennis

During the summer of 1968, women's tennis champion Billie Jean King was trying to put together events that would help professional tennis players make more money. To do this Billie Jean organized tennis tournaments starring older big-name tennis players. People, she hoped, would pay to see the "stars" of the sport, even if they were a bit past their prime. If this could be accomplished, tennis players would be able to play tennis for a living for years after they stopped making the finals at Wimbledon. Althea was in the middle of her golf career when Billie Jean called her. Would Althea like to play in a tournament at the Coliseum Arena in Oakland? The money wasn't much, a total of $5,000 to go around. But if the event were successful, it might be a big step toward establishing a "Stars of Tennis" tour. Althea was 41 years old.

Billie Jean said, "If you are worried about embarrassing yourself, you don't have to come."

That was the sort of challenge that Althea could not refuse. She played in the Oakland event, and, although she did not win a match, she had a great time. It was great to hear the applause from a tennis crowd again. She told Billie Jean that if she ever held a similar event, she shouldn't hesitate to give her a call. She would love to do it again. She then returned to the golf tour, where things were still not looking up.

Althea had dreamed of becoming a top world golfer, and it was now clear that this was not going to happen. She owed more to the bank to repay the loans than she figured to make on the golf course. She would never make a profit playing golf.

Socially, Althea's move to integrate women's golf was a huge success. She had again battered down the social barriers put in the path of all African Americans. But, as an attempt to make a living, golf had been a failure for Althea.

And so, in 1971, she retired as a pro golfer. Althea was pleased to find that many of the color barriers in country clubs were falling. Clubs that wouldn't have thought of hiring her 10 or 15 years before now offered Althea jobs.

Last Days on the Court

In 1972, Althea noted that professional women's tennis was stronger than ever. There were at least three women—Billie Jean King, Margaret Court, and Evonne Goolagong—who were making good money. Althea was now 44 years old, but she refused to believe that her glory days were behind her. She told one reporter that she yearned once again to "be associated with the sport that made me famous."

She told *The Sporting News* during a golf tournament that she was planning a tennis comeback, maybe playing doubles. "The opportunities in tennis now are greater than they've ever been," she said. "The girls are playing for large sums of money. Now the money in tennis provides an opportunity for a girl to make a fair living out of the sport. Maybe if I concentrate on it, I might even get a piece of it."

Billed as Althea Gibson Darben, Althea teamed up with Gar Malloy to play mixed doubles that year at Forest Hills. They won their first set but lost their first match and were eliminated.

A year later, Althea tried one last time to play competitive tennis. She once again entered the Forest Hills tournament in the mixed doubles division. This time her partner was Arthur Ashe. Only four times had a singles championship at Forest Hills been won by an African American, and Althea and Arthur were responsible for all of them. Althea was really showing her age now, however. Even though Ashe played very well, Althea did not, and they lost 6-2, 6-2 in their opening match. That was Althea's last attempt at serious competitive tennis.

7

TIME TO TEACH

Having retired from both tennis and golf, Althea needed another way to make money. She decided that it was time to use the wisdom of her years, time to pass on her knowledge to a new generation. She decided to become a teacher.

For a time she worked as a special sports consultant for the Essex County, New Jersey, Park Commission. She gave tennis and golf lessons to groups of youngsters. The kids looked upon her as a hero. She got great satisfaction from the job, giving hope and ambition to kids who otherwise might have been held back by despair.

She was delighted to learn that by 1971 it was no longer impossible for a black woman to be hired by a country club. In fact, for a woman of Althea's accomplishments, it was easy. She received several job offers.

She picked a job close to home, so she would be able to spend as much time with Will as possible. Althea became a professional tennis teacher at a New Jersey country club. She practically lived on the tennis court in her new job, giving lessons and volleying with the club members. Althea and the members of the club quickly discovered that she was still a very good tennis player.

Around this time, the days of amateur tennis were coming to a close. Althea learned that women's tennis tournaments were now paying good money. Thus, she was strongly tempted to re-enter the world of competitive tennis.

In 1971 Althea applied to play in the U.S. Open at Forest Hills. She assumed that, as a former winner of the tournament, she would automatically be allowed to play. In golf, for example, a winner of the Masters' Tournament gets to play in the tournament every year from then on without having to qualify. But that was not the case at Forest Hills. Althea was told that she would have to win a qualifying tournament to play in the big tournament.

Althea was offended by the treatment she received at Forest Hills. She also feared that she was too old to play at this level. She might lose in the qualifier to a tennis player no one had heard of. She was afraid of embarrassing herself by coming back when her skills were shot. So she backed out. She decided that she didn't want to play at Forest Hills that badly after all.

Althea may have quit playing golf professionally, but she did not give up the game entirely. Now that she was no longer struggling to be the best lady golfer in the world, she once again found that golf relaxed her. Althea's time on the golf course again helped her forget her troubles.

After a few months working at the country club, she was able to pay off all of her loans. No longer worried about being in debt, Althea again desired to be in business for herself. She had once quit her job with the Harlem Globetrotters to start her own traveling tennis tour. Now she quit her job at the country club to open her own tennis club. It was an indoor club, and when it opened one sports columnist in the newspaper said it was "beautiful." At first it did great business. Althea's name attracted the curious.

Recognition

During the 1970s, Althea's contributions to sports and to society were recognized again and again. In 1971 she was inducted into two Halls of Fame: the National Lawn Tennis Hall of Fame in Newport, Rhode Island, (the organization is now known as the International Tennis Hall of Fame) and the International Sportsman Hall of Fame. In

1974, Althea became a member of the Black Athletes Hall of Fame.

But there were problems during the decade as well. In 1975 Althea's indoor tennis club wasn't doing nearly the business it had done when it first opened four years before. Now the place was empty. Althea was forced to go out of business and close the place down. That same year Althea divorced Will Darben. They had been married for 10 years.

In need of work, in 1975 Althea took a job as the Department of Recreation manager in East Orange, New Jersey. As she had back in 1970 when working as a consultant for the Essex County Park Commission in New Jersey, she enjoyed working with the inner-city kids. Many of the youngsters reminded her of herself and her friends growing up in Harlem.

She put much time and energy into helping young people develop into better athletes and people that she became a beloved member of the community. Before 1975 was over, Gibson had been named New Jersey's state commissioner of athletics.

Twilight of an Athletic Career

Althea played tennis in front of a paying audience for one of the last times in 1974. The ladies' finals had to be canceled at the last second when one of the women hurt her toe and had to withdraw. To give the crowd something to

Later in her career, Althea devoted much of her time to helping young people develop their athletic abilities.
(Associated Press)

watch, the promoters asked Althea if she would play an exhibition match against Chris Evert, who, though still a teenager, was one of the best tennis players in the world. Althea agreed, adding that she intended to win. "Chrissy," as Evert was known, defeated Althea 6-1 and went out of her way not to make the older woman look bad. Afterward, Althea said she could have won the match if only she'd had time to get in shape.

Althea did get another chance to showcase her athletic skills in 1976. At that time there was a TV show called *Superstars*, which pitted athletes from various sports in a series of 10 competitions. The winner of the most points won a lot of money and was named best overall athlete.

Billie Jean King had been asked to be part of the competition and agreed to be the show's color commentator if Althea Gibson was allowed to be one of the competitors. Billie Jean worried that Althea's athletic and social accomplishments were being forgotten. This show, Billie Jean thought, would put 49-year-old Althea in the spotlight one more time.

Among the other competitors were tennis star Martina Navratilova, golfers Jane Blalock and Amy Alcott; drag racer Shirley Muldowney; diver Micki King; distance swimmer Diana Nyad; surfer Laura Ching; speed skater Anne Henning; skier Kiki Cutter; and track star Wyomia

Tyus. Most of the women were more than 20 years younger than Althea.

According to biographer Bruce Schoenfeld, there were more people watching Althea on TV during this show than had previously seen her play all of her tennis and golf combined.

Althea provided an early highlight on the show when she won the bowling event. She still had the fine form she had shown so many years before in the late-night bowling alleys of Harlem.

Then Althea won the *Superstars* basketball-shooting contest. Althea recalled the many hours she had spent shooting baskets during her youth. Some of those practice sessions took place under lights while the rest of the world slept, Althea and Gloria Nightingale knocking down jump-shots in the playgrounds of 143rd Street. It all came in handy on national TV.

Bowling and basketball were the high-points of her TV effort. Althea struggled in some of the other events, such as the 60-meter dash and the obstacle course. Anne Henning, the speed skater, won the overall contest—and the first-place prize money: $30,000. Althea finished in the top 10 and was pleased to receive a check for $4,200. After that, she thanked Billie Jean King again and again for getting her the *Superstars* opportunity.

In 1978 Althea told a reporter that she still hadn't given up on the idea of a golf comeback. She tried to qualify to play in that year's 1978 LPGA Championship in Mason, Ohio. She didn't make it.

"I am closer than most people think," Althea said after she failed to qualify. She never was one to admit defeat. But inside she must have accepted it. She never tried again.

"There will never be another Althea Gibson"

In 1980 one newspaper reporter wrote about Althea: "There will never be another Althea Gibson. To meet with and talk with this woman is to learn a little bit about what it takes to be a champion."

Althea served on the State Athletics Control Board until 1988 and on the Governor's Council on Physical Fitness until 1992.

The 1980s brought more honors. In 1983, she was inducted into the South Carolina Hall of Fame. The following year, she was inducted into the Florida Sports Hall of Fame. Together with longtime friend Fran Gray, Althea formed the Althea Gibson Foundation in 1998, which helped urban youths learn to play tennis and golf.

In 1988 Althea presented her Wimbledon trophies to the Smithsonian Institution in Washington, D.C. At the ceremony, Althea said, "Who could have imagined? Who could have thought? Here stands before you a Negro woman, raised in Harlem, who went on to become a tennis player . . . in fact, the first black woman champion of this world."

In 1990 Althea told a *Sports Illustrated* reporter that she was still considering a golf comeback. "Her chances of success are a longshot at best," the reporter wrote, "but it is hard to find anybody who isn't pulling for her."

In 1991 Althea worked several jobs, as a New Jersey State Athletic Commissioner and serving on the New Jersey Governor's Council on Physical Fitness and Sports.

Also in 1991, Althea received the NCAA's Theodore Roosevelt Award (called the "Teddy") for her contribution to collegiate athletics. The award was given once a year to the former college athlete who had used his or her skills to create the greatest national impact. Althea was now used to breaking down social barriers. She was proud but not surprised when she learned that this was the 85th year that the "Teddy" had been presented. The previous 84 had gone to men. Althea was the first woman ever to receive it.

However, Althea was not pleased at the rate at which the tennis world was integrating. There were always a few black tennis players among the world's best during any give year but never more than a few. After Althea came African-American tennis players such as Zina Garrison Jackson, Lori McNeil, the great champion Arthur Ashe, Chandra Rubin, and the Williams sisters, Venus and Serena.

In 1990 Althea publicly showed her support for Zina Garrison, who reached the finals at Wimbledon before losing to Martina Navratilova. Zina was the first African-American woman to make it to the finals at Wimbledon since Althea had done so 32 years before.

In 1991, writer Sue Davidson wrote of Althea: "Althea maintains an intense interest in tennis. She has promoted the welfare of the sport in general and the progress of young black players in particular."

She remained active with the ATA, the black tennis association that had sanctioned the young Althea's first tournaments as a player.

Loss of a Role Model

In 1991 Alice Marble died. Marble was the woman who had come to the Cosmopolitan Club to play an exhibition match when Althea was a teenager just learning the game. It was Marble's aggressive, hard-hitting style of tennis that had shaped Althea's own game. Marble showed the world that women's tennis could be just as strong and competitive as the men's game and just as much fun to watch. Plus, Marble had taken such a strong civil rights stand when Althea was trying to break the color barrier in women's tennis.

Althea once wrote, "My story is an example of how much Miss Marble has done for fair play in sports."

As one writer put it, Alice "opened doors through which Althea charged."

Althea had always been impressed with Alice's sense of fair play, of course, but she had also been impressed with the way Alice was always willing to pass on her wisdom to the generations of tennis players who followed her. Althea was determined to do the same for as long as she could.

And so Althea continued to be a tennis teacher until, in the mid-1990s, she suffered a stroke and was in declining health. During Althea's long illness, she struggled financially. In 1996, Althea's struggles became public. Donations to help her pay her medical bills poured in. One of those donations was $200 from Marian de Swardt, a South African tennis player.

"I focused on your game when I learned how to play, and I wanted to thank you," a note from de Swardt read.

In 2002, at the U.S. Open tennis tournament in Flushing, New York, a ceremony was held to commemorate Althea's 75th birthday. Sadly, as a result of her declining health, Althea was not able to attend the ceremony.

"She broke down a lot of barriers and doors"

Althea died on September 28, 2003, at age 76. Her funeral was held on October 2, 2003, at St. Phillip's Trinity Episcopal Church in Newark, New Jersey. In her autobiography, she wrote: "I always wanted to be somebody. If I

Through her long and distinguished career, Althea Gibson set records and broke new ground for African Americans in professional sports.

made it, it's half because I was game enough to take a lot of punishment along the way and half because there were a lot of people who cared enough to help me."

Upon hearing of Gibson's death, African-American tennis star Venus Williams said, "I am grateful to Althea Gibson for having the strength and courage to break through the racial barriers in tennis. Her accomplishments set the stage for my success, and through players like myself, [my sister] Serena, and many others to come, her legacy will live on. Gibson was the first African-American woman to rank number-one and win Wimbledon, and I am honored to have followed in such great footsteps."

Martina Navratilova said, "Her life was very difficult, but she broke down a lot of barriers and doors and made it easier for a lot of us."

Billie Jean King, a Grand Slam champion who helped found the Women's Tennis Association, told the press that she was 13 when she first saw Gibson play: "It was truly an inspiration for me to watch her overcome adversity. Her road to success was a challenging one, but I never saw her back down. Althea did a lot for people in tennis, but she did even more for people in general."

"Her contribution to the civil rights movement was done with her tennis racket," said Althea's longtime friend and co-founder of the Althea Gibson Foundation, Fran Gray. "Althea came up in a hard time. Segregation was no easy thing. It was a feat that she accomplished under really devastating and debilitating odds because she wasn't wanted."

Althea did not dwell on what she referred to as "the color question." After winning at Forest Hills and Wimbledon, she no longer felt excluded—not from anything that mattered anyway.

"Maybe I can't stay overnight at a good hotel in Columbia, South Carolina," she said in 1958, "or play a tennis match against a white opponent in Louisiana. But I can get along without sleeping in that hotel, and I don't care if I never set foot in Louisiana. There is, I have found out, a whole lot of world outside Louisiana . . . I'm not a racially conscious person. I see myself as just an individual. I'm a tennis player, not a Negro tennis player."

When people look back at Althea's life, they see much more than the story of a talented tennis player who rose to become the best in the world. They see a groundbreaking African-American woman. Like Jackie Robinson before her, Althea bravely broke the color barrier—in both tennis and golf. She allowed people of color to compete against their white counterparts. The rules changed in country clubs around the country and the world.

It was her need to be "somebody" that, as she put it, "made me live like a gypsy" for all those years. "It has been a bewildering, challenging, exhausting experience, often more painful than pleasurable, more sad than happy," she said in the late 1950s. "But I wouldn't have missed it for the world."

TIME LINE

1927   Born on August 25 in Silver, South Carolina

1930   Moves to New York City

1941   Begins tennis lessons at the Cosmopolitan Club in Harlem

1942   Wins first tennis tournament, an all-black event sanctioned by the American Tennis Association

1946   Begins tennis lessons with Dr. Hubert A. Eaton in Wilmington, North Carolina

1947   Wins first of 10 ATA National Championships

1949   Enrolls at Florida A&M University; plays against white players for the first time

1950   First plays in the U.S. National Tennis Championship, in Forest Hills, New York

1951   First plays in the All-England Tennis Championship at Wimbledon

1953   Graduates from Florida A&M

1954   Moves to Jefferson City, Missouri; begins lessons with tennis coach Sydney Llewellyn

1955–
1956   Tours Southeast Asia for the U.S. State Department

1956   Wins the French Championships; plays several tournaments in Australia

1957   Wins both the U.S. National Tennis Championship, in Forest Hills, New York, and the All-England Tennis Championship at Wimbledon

1958   For the second year in a row wins both at Wimbledon and at Forest Hills; retires as an amateur tennis player

1959   Makes acting debut in movie *The Horse Soldiers*; makes professional singing debut with release of album *Althea Gibson Sings*

1960   Playing exhibition tennis, tours with the Harlem Globetrotters basketball team

1964   Becomes a pro golfer and plays in tournaments sanctioned by the Ladies Professional Golf Association

1965 Marries Will Darben in Las Vegas, Nevada

1971 Retires as a pro golfer; becomes a professional tennis teacher; is inducted into the National Lawn Tennis Hall of Fame, now known as the International Tennis Hall of Fame

1974 Is inducted into the Black Athletes Hall of Fame

1975 Divorces Will Darben; becomes Department of Recreation manager in East Orange, New Jersey

1983 Is inducted into the South Carolina Hall of Fame, in Myrtle Beach, South Carolina

1984 Is inducted into the Florida Sports Hall of Fame in Lake City, Florida; marries and divorces Sydney Llewellyn, so her long-time coach/manager can get his U.S. citizenship

1991 Appointed to the New Jersey State Athletic Commission; serves on the New Jersey Governor's Council on Physical Fitness and Sports; receives the NCAA's Theodore Roosevelt Award for her contribution to collegiate athletics

Mid- Suffers stroke; is in declining health
1990s

2003 Dies on September 28 at the age of 76

HOW TO BECOME A PROFESSIONAL ATHLETE

THE JOB

Professional athletes participate in individual sports such as tennis, figure-skating, golf, running, or boxing, competing against others to win prizes and money.

Depending on the nature of the specific sport, most athletes compete against a field of individuals. The field of competitors can be as small as one (tennis, boxing) or as large as the number of qualified competitors, anywhere from six to 30 (figure skating, golf, cycling). In certain individual events, such as the marathon or triathlon, the field may seem excessively large—often tens of thousands of runners compete in the New York Marathon—but for the professional runners competing in the race, only a handful of other runners represent real competition.

The athletic performances of those in individual sports are evaluated according to the nature and rules of each specific sport. For example, the winner of a foot race is whoever crosses the finish line first; in tennis the winner is the one who scores the highest in a set number of games; in boxing and figure skating, the winners are determined by a panel of judges. Competitions are organized by local, regional, national, and international organizations and associations whose primary functions are to promote the sport and sponsor competitive events. Within a professional sport there are usually different levels of competition based on age, ability, and gender. There are often different designations and events within one sport. Tennis, for example, consists of doubles and singles, while track and field contains many different events, from field events such as the javelin and shot putt, to track events such as the 110-meter dash and the two-mile relay race.

Athletes train year-round, on their own or with a coach, friend, parent, or trainer. In addition to stretching and exercising the specific muscles used in any given sport, athletes concentrate on developing excellent eating and sleeping habits that will help them remain in top condition throughout the year. Although certain sports have a particular season, most professional athletes train rigorously all year, varying the type and duration of their workouts to develop strength, cardiovascular ability, flexibility, endurance, speed, and quickness, as well as to focus on technique and control. Often, an athlete's training focuses less on the overall game or program that the athlete will execute, than on specific areas or details of that game or program. Figure skaters, for example, won't simply keep going through their entire long programs from start to finish but instead will focus on the jumps, turns, and hand movements that refine the program. Similarly, sprinters don't keep running only the sprint distances they race in during a meet; instead, they vary their workouts to include some distance work, some sprints, a lot of weight training to build strength, and maybe some mental exercises to build control and focus while in the starter's blocks. Tennis players routinely spend hours just practicing their forehand, down-the-line shots.

Athletes often watch videotapes or films of their previous practices or competitions to see where they can improve their performance. They also study what the other competitors are doing in order to prepare strategies for winning.

REQUIREMENTS

High School

A high school diploma will provide you with the basic skills that you will need in your long climb to becoming a professional athlete. Business and mathematics classes will teach you how to manage money wisely. Speech classes will help you become a better communicator. Physical education classes will help you build your strength, agility, and competitive spirit. You should, of course, participate in every organized sport that your school offers and that interests you.

Some individual sports such as tennis and gymnastics have professional competitors who are high school students. Teenagers in this situation often have private coaches with whom they practice both before and after going to school, and others are home-schooled as they travel to competitions.

Postsecondary Training

There are no formal education requirements for sports, although certain competitions and training opportunities are only available to those enrolled in four-year colleges and universities. Collegiate-level competitions are where most athletes in this area hone their skills; they may also compete in international or national competitions outside of college, but the chance to train and receive an education isn't one many serious athletes refuse. In fact, outstanding ability in athletics is the way many students pay for their college educations. Given the chances of striking it rich financially, an education (especially a free one) is a wise investment and one fully supported by most professional sports organizations.

Other Requirements

There is so much competition to be among the world's elite athletes in any given sport that talent alone isn't the primary requirement. Diligence, perseverance, hard work, ambition, and courage are all essential qualities to the individual who dreams of making a career as a professional athlete. "If you want to be a pro, there's no halfway. There's no three-quarters way," says Eric Roller, a former professional tennis player who competed primarily on the Florida circuit. Other, specific requirements will vary according to the sport. Jockeys, for example, are usually petite men and women.

EXPLORING

If you are interested in pursuing a career in professional sports you should start participating in that sport as much and as early as possible. With some sports, an individual who is 15 may already be too old to realistically begin pursuing a professional career. By playing the sport and by talking to coaches, trainers, and athletes in the field, you can ascertain whether you like the sport enough to make it a career, determine if you have enough talent, and gain new insight into the field. You can also contact professional organizations and associations for information on how to best prepare for a career in their sport. Sometimes there are specialized training programs available, and the best way to find out is to get in contact with the people whose job it is to promote the sport.

EMPLOYERS

Professional athletes who compete in individual sports are not employed in the same manner as most workers. They do not work for employers, but choose the competitions or tournaments they wish to compete in. For example, a professional runner may choose to enter the Boston Marathon and then travel to Atlanta for the Peachtree Road Race.

STARTING OUT

Professional athletes must meet the requirements established by the organizing bodies of their respective sport. Sometimes this means meeting a physical requirement, such as age, height, or weight; and sometimes this means fulfilling a number of required stunts, or participating in a certain number of competitions. Professional organizations usually arrange it so that athletes can build up their skills and level of play by participating in lower-level competitions. College sports, as mentioned earlier, are an excellent way to improve one's skills while pursuing an education.

ADVANCEMENT

Professional athletes advance into the elite numbers of their sport by working and practicing hard, and by winning. Professional athletes usually obtain representation by sports agents in the behind-the-scenes deals that determine for which teams they will be playing and what they will be paid. These agents may also be involved with other key decisions involving commercial endorsements, personal income taxes, and financial investments of the athlete's revenues.

A college education can prepare all athletes for the day when their bodies can no longer compete at the top level, whether because of age or an unforeseen injury. Every athlete should be prepared to move into another career, related to the world of sports or not.

EARNINGS

The U.S. Department of Labor reports that athletes had median annual earnings of $45,780 in 2003. Ten percent earned less than $13,310.

Salaries, prize monies, and commercial endorsements will vary from sport to sport; a lot depends on the popularity of the sport and its ability to attract spectators, or on the sport's professional organization and its ability to drum up sponsors for competitions and prize money. Still other sports, like boxing, depend on the skill of the fight's promoters to create interest in the fight. An elite professional tennis player who wins Wimbledon, for example, usually earns more than half a million dollars in a matter of several hours. Add to that the incredible sums a Wimbledon-champion can make in endorsements and the tennis star can earn more than one million dollars a year. This scenario is misleading, however; to begin with, top athletes usually cannot perform at such a level for very long, which is why a good accountant and investment counselor comes in handy. Secondly, for every top athlete who earns millions of dollars in a year, there are hundreds of professional athletes who earn less than $40,000. The stakes are incredibly high, the competition fierce.

Perhaps the only caveat to the financial success of an elite athlete is the individual's character or personality. An athlete with a bad temper or prone to unsportsmanlike behavior may still be able to set records or win games, but he or she won't necessarily be able to cash in on commercial endorsements. Advertisers are notoriously fickle about the spokespeople they choose to endorse products;

some athletes have lost million-dollar accounts because of their bad behavior on and off the field of play.

Other options exist, thankfully, for professional athletes. Many go into some area of coaching, sports administration, management, or broadcasting. The professional athlete's unique insight and perspective can be a real asset in careers in these areas. Other athletes have been simultaneously pursuing other interests, some completely unrelated to their sport, such as education, business, social welfare, or the arts. Many continue to stay involved with the sport they have loved since childhood, coaching young children or volunteering with local school teams.

WORK ENVIRONMENT

Athletes compete in many different conditions, according to the setting of the sport (indoors or outdoors) and the rules of the organizing or governing bodies. Track-and-field athletes often compete in hot or rainy conditions, but at any point, organizing officials can call off the meet, or postpone competition until better weather. Indoor events are less subject to cancellation. However, since it is in the best interests of an organization not to risk the athletes' health, any condition that might adversely affect the outcome of a competition is usually reason enough to cancel or postpone it. An athlete, on the other hand, may withdraw from competition if he or she is injured or ill. Nerves and fear are not good reasons to default on a competition and part of ascending into the ranks of professional athletes means learning to cope with the anxiety that competition brings. Some athletes actually thrive on the nervous tension.

In order to reach the elite level of any sport, athletes must begin their careers early. Most professional athletes have been working at their sports since they were small children; skiers, figure skaters, and gymnasts, for example, begin skiing, skating, and tumbling as young as age two or three. Athletes have to fit hours of practice time into an already full day, usually several hours before school, and several hours after school. To make the situation more difficult, competitions and facilities for practice are often far from the young athlete's home, which means they either commute to and from practice and competitions with a parent, or they live with a coach or trainer for most of the year. Separation from a child's parents and family is an especially hard and frustrating element of the training program. When a child has demonstrated uncommon excellence in a sport, the family often decides to move to the city in which the sports facility is located, so that the child doesn't have to travel or be separated from a normal family environment.

The expenses of a sport can be overwhelming, as can the time an athlete must devote to practice and travel to and from competitions. In addition to specialized equipment and clothing, the athlete must pay for a coach, travel expenses, competition fees and, depending on the sport, time at the facility or gym where he or she practices. Tennis, golf, figure skating, and skiing are among the most expensive sports to enter.

Even with the years of hard work, practice, and financial sacrifice that most athletes and their families must endure, there is no guarantee that an athlete will achieve the rarest of the rare in the sports world—financial reward. An athlete needs to truly love the sport at which he or she excels, and also have a nearly insatiable ambition and work ethic.

OUTLOOK

The outlook for professional athletes will vary depending on the sport, its popularity, and the number of athletes currently competing. On the whole, the outlook for the field of professional sports is healthy, but the number of jobs will not increase dramatically. Some sports, however, may experience an increase in popularity, which will translate into greater opportunities for higher salaries, prize monies, and commercial endorsements.

TO LEARN MORE ABOUT PROFESSIONAL ATHLETES

BOOKS

Benson, Michael. *Hank Aaron: Baseball Player.* Ferguson Career Biographies. New York: Ferguson, 2005.

Denenberg, Barry. *Stealing Home: The Story of Jackie Robinson.* New York: Scholastic, 1997.

Gutman, Bill. *Venus & Serena: The Grand Slam Williams Sisters.* New York: Scholastic, 2001.

Martin, Marvin. *Arthur Ashe: Of Tennis and the Human Spirit.* New York: Franklin Watts, 1999.

Williams, Venus, and Serena Williams. *How to Play Tennis.* New York: DK Publishing, 2004.

WEBSITES

Individuals interested in becoming professional athletes should contact the professional organizations for the sport in which they would like to compete, such as the National Tennis Association, the Professional Golf Association, or the National Bowling Association. Ask for information on requirements, training centers, and coaches. The following organization may also be able to provide further information:

American Alliance for Health, Physical Education, Recreation, and Dance

1900 Association Drive

Reston, VA 20191-1598

Tel: 800-213-7193

http://www.aahperd.org

For a free brochure and information on the Junior Olympics and more, contact

Amateur Athletic Union

PO Box 22409

Lake Buena Vista, FL 32830

Tel: 407-934-7200

http://www.aausports.org

TO LEARN MORE ABOUT ALTHEA GIBSON AND TENNIS

BOOKS

Aaseng, Nathan. *Winning Women of Tennis.* Minneapolis, Minnesota: Lerner Publications, 1981.

Ashe, Arthur R., Jr. *A Hard Road to Glory: A History of the African-American Athlete 1619-1918*. New York: Warner Books, 1988.

——. *A Hard Road to Glory: A History of the African-American Athlete 1919-1945.* New York: Warner Books, 1988.

Biracree, Tom. *Althea Gibson*. Los Angeles, California: Melrose Square Publishing Company, 1990.

Davidson, Sue. *Changing the Game: The Stories of Tennis Champions Alice Marble & Althea Gibson*. Seattle, Washington: Seal Press, 1997.

Gibson, Althea. *I Always Wanted to Be Somebody*. New York: Harper & Brothers, 1958.

———. *So Much to Live For*. New York: Putnam, 1968.

Grimsley, Will. *Tennis: Its History, People and Events*. Englewood-Cliffs, New Jersey: Prentice-Hall, 1971.

Hollander, Phyllis. *American Women in Sports*. New York: Grosset & Dunlap, 1972.

King, Billie Jean. *We Have Come a Long Way*. New York: McGraw-Hill, 1988.

Lichtenstein, Grace. *A Long Way, Baby: Behind the Scenes in Women's Pro Tennis*. New York: Morrow, 1974.

Lumpkin, Angela. *Women's Tennis: A Historical Documentary of the Players and Their Game*. Troy, New York: Whitston Publications, 1981.

Ryan, Joan. *Contributions of Women: Sports*. Minneapolis, Minnesota: Dillon Press, 1975.

Schoenfeld, Bruce. *The Match: Althea Gibson & Angela Buxton*. New York: HarperCollins, 2004.

Sullivan, George. *Queens of the Court*. New York: Dodd, Mead, 1974.

WEBSITES

Ross, Ashley. "Legend and Pioneer Althea Gibson Remembered." *The Hilltop* (electronic version of the Howard University student newspaper). Available online. URL: http://www.thehilltoponline.com. Posted October 3, 2003.

ORGANIZATIONS

Florida Sports Hall of Fame

601 Hall of Fame Drive

Lake City, Florida

Phone: (386) 758-1310

Toll free: (800) 352-3263

Located just off Highway 90 West, the hall of fame is open 9:00 A.M. to 4:00 P.M. Tuesday through Saturday. Admission is $3.00.

International Tennis Hall of Fame

194 Bellevue Avenue

Newport, Rhode Island 02840

Phone: 401-849-3990, 800-457-1144

Fax: 401-849-8780

Email: newport@tennisfame.com

http://www.tennisfame.com

As Allison Danzig said in 1955: "The Hall of Fame is something more than a lovely physical property. It is an inspiration for the young, setting them a goal that can only be attained through the sacrifice, perseverance and strength of character that won a place for those already enshrined there. Sport still has its ideals. None are loftier than those represented by The Tennis Hall of Fame."

South Carolina Hall of Fame

Myrtle Beach Convention Center

2100 Oak Street

Myrtle Beach, South Carolina

Phone: (843) 918-1225 ext. 1252

The South Carolina Hall of Fame is located in the "Hall of Fame Lobby" and is open daily from 8:30 A.M. to 5:00 P.M. There is no admission charge.

TENNIS GLOSSARY

Advantage   The player who scores the first point after deuce is said to have the advantage, since winning the next point will also win the game; sometimes shortened to "Ad."

Back court   Area of the court from the baseline to the service line.

Backhand   Shot hit from the side of the body away from the racket; the left side for a right-handed player.

Baseline   A line at the end of the court, parallel to the net, that marks the lengthwise boundary of the playing area.

Center service line   A line extending from the net to the midpoint of the service line that marks the boundary for both service courts.

Court   Seventy-eight foot by 27-foot rectangle marked off on a grass, clay or paved surface, divided across the middle by the net. Service lines are marked 21 feet from each side of the net and parallel to it. The area bounded by the singles sidelines and the service line is divided into two equal parts, the service courts, by the center service line, which is halfway between the sidelines and parallel to them.

Deuce   A tie.

Double fault   When the server fails at both attempts at a valid serve, it is a double fault and the receiver wins the point.

Game   A contest in which one player or side serves throughout. The first contestant to take four points wins the game—following the scoring sequence 15, 30, 40, Game—but the margin of victory must be at least two points.

Hold serve   Game in which the winner is serving.

Let   A do-over. A stroke that doesn't count and must be replayed. This most commonly happens when a serve hits the top of the net before landing in the proper service court.

Love   Zero.

Match   A tennis contest made up of sets, as a set is made up of games. Men's matches are usually best of five sets, with the first player to win three sets being the victor. Women play best of three sets.

Out Shot that lands outside the playing area, wide and/or long, is out.

Point One volley played to a conclusion. Four points win a game.

Racket Tool used to strike the ball. Rackets may be as long as 29 1/2 inches in overall length, and 12 1/2 inches in overall width. The hitting surface can be no more than 15 1/2 inches long and 11 1/2 inches wide.

Serve Shot that starts each point. Standing behind the baseline, the player must toss the ball into the air and hit it into the diagonally opposite service court. The server is given two chances to make a valid serve.

Set First player to win six games wins the set. In women's tennis the first player to win two sets wins the match. Today's sets that tie at 6-6 are ended with a tiebreaker. When Althea Gibson played, sets had to be won by at least two games, resulting in very long sets with scored such as 10-8 and 12-10.

USLTA United States Lawn Tennis Association.

INDEX

Page numbers in *italics* indicate photographs.

A

Alcott, Amy 98
All-Asian Tennis Tournament 50
All-England Tennis Championship 41, 110
    See also Wimbledon Tournament
Althea Gibson Benefit Show 42
Althea Gibson Enterprises Inc. 79–80
Althea Gibson Foundation 100, 105
Althea Gibson Show 79–80
Althea Gibson Sings (album) 77, 110
Amateur Athletic Union (AAU) 126
American Alliance for Health, Physical Education, Recreation, and Dance 126
American Lawn Tennis 31
American Tennis Association (ATA) 14, 18, 19, 22, 23, 26, 28, 41, 43, 64, 102, 109
Ashe, Arthur 72, 92, 101
ATA. *See* American Tennis Association (ATA)

athletes, professional
    advancement 119
    books about 125
    earnings 119–121
    employers 118
    exploring 117–118
    high school and postsecondary training 116–117
    job overview 113–115
    organizations and websites about 126
    outlook 123
    starting out 118–119
    work environment 121–123

B

Babe Didrikson Zaharias Trophy 66, 73
Black Athletes Hall of Fame 95–96, 111
Blalock, Jane 98
Bloomer, Shirley 70
Brough, Louise 36–38, 39–40, 69
Brown, Jim 62
Buxton, Angela 51–53, 55–56, 64

C

Chaffee, Nancy 27, 29
Ching, Laura 98
Churchill, Winston 63
Cosmopolitan Club 13–18, 30, 102, 109
Court, Margaret 91
Cutter, Kiki 98

D

Danzig, Allison 130
Darben, Althea Gibson 92
    See also Gibson, Althea
Darben, Rosemary 45, 88
Darben, Will 45, 88–89, 94, 96, 111
Davidson, Sue 102
Davis, Nana 18
de Swardt, Marian 103
Dot Records 77

E

Eaton, Hubert A. 22–24, 25, 26, 64, 109
Ed Sullivan Show (TV program) 77
Eisenhower, Dwight D. 62–63
Elizabeth II, queen of England 60, 61–62, 64, 72
Englewood Golf Club 84
Essex County, New Jersey, Park Commission 93, 96
Evert, Chris 98

F

Fageros, Karol 49, 50, 69, 78
Florida A&M University 28, 29, 40, 43, 75, 109, 110
Florida Sports Hall of Fame 100, 111, 129
Flushing tournament 103
    See also U.S. Open
Forest Hills tournament 26
    1950 33, 35, 36–40, *37,* 109

1954 44
1955 47, 49
1956 56
1957 69, 106, 110
1958 73, 110
1971 94–95
1972 92
1973 92
1974 96, 98
    See also U.S. National Tennis Championship; U.S. Open
French Championships (1956) 51, 53
Fry, Shirley 54, 56, 57

G

Garrison, Zina 72, 102
    See also Jackson, Zina Garrison
Gibson, Althea *4, 10*
    as actor 76, 110
    "Althea Gibson Benefit Show" for 42
    in Althea Gibson Show 79–80
    army plans of 46–47, 49
    in Asian tournaments 49–51, 57, 110
    in ATA tournaments 14, 18, 19, 22, 23, 26, 28, 43, 109
    autobiography 55–56, 70, 103, 105
    birth 1, 109
    books about 127–128
    Buxton and 51–53, 55–56, 64
    in Caribbean and South American tournaments 66
    childhood 1–8
    in college 28–30, 40, 43, 75, 109, 110
    as consultant for Essex County, New Jersey, Park Commission 96

at Cosmopolitan Club 13–18, 109

as Department of Recreation manager 96, *97,* 111

Drs. Eaton and Johnson and 22–26, 64, 109

in Eastern and National Indoor Championships 27

on equal rights and racism 23, 24–25, 26–27, 28, 30–33, 35, 40–41, 53–55, 67–68, 74, 86, 87, 89, 91, 101, 102, 105–107

at Forest Hills 33, 35, 36–40, *37,* 44, 47, 49, 56, 69, 73, 92, 94–95, 96, 98, 103, 106, 109, 110

in French Championships 51–53, 110

as golfer 58, 82–89, *85,* 90–91, 95, 100, 101, 110, 111

with Harlem Globetrotters 77–79, 110

in high school 8, 24, 26, 28, 75

illness and death 103, 111

King and 89–90, 98, 99, 105

Llewellyn and 45–46, 64, 75, 79, 110, 111

Louis and 42

Marble and 17, 30–31, *32,* 36, 102–103

marriage to Darben and divorce 88–89, 96, 111

on New Jersey Governor's Council on Physical Fitness and Sports 100, 101, 111

as New Jersey State Athletic Commissioner 96, 100, 101, 111

organizations and websites about 129–130

on paddle tennis 9–11

recognition of 56–57, 61–63, 64, *65,* 66, 73, 78, 95–96, 100–101, *104,* 105–106, 111

Robinson and 20–22, *21*

as singer 24, 74–77, 110

as spokesperson for Tip Top Bread 81–82, 86

on *Superstars* 98–99

as teacher 44, 93–94, 95, *97,* 103, 111

as teenager 8–19

tennis club of 95, 96

time line 109–111

at Wimbledon 41, 42–43, 53–56, 58–66, *60, 65,* 70–72, *71,* 110

Gibson, Annie 1, 2, 3, *4,* 66, 79

Gibson, Daniel 1, 2, 3, *4,* 5, 8, 79

Globetrotters. *See* Harlem Globetrotters

Goolagong, Evonne 91

Gray, Fran 100, 105–106

H

Hall, Scottie 54–55

Handy, W. C. 76

Hard, Darlene 61, 73

Harlem Globetrotters 77–78, 79, 95, 110

Harriman, Averill 62

Haydon, Ann 70

Henning, Anne 98, 99

Hill, Edward 62

Hoad, Lew 64

Horse Soldiers, The (film) 76, 110

Howard University 62, 129

Hoxie, Jean 42

I

I Always Wanted to Be Somebody (Gibson) 70

International Sportsman Hall of
Fame 95
International Tennis Hall of Fame
95, 111, 129–130

J

Jackson, Zina Garrison 101
See also Garrison, Zina
Jet 44
Johnson, Fred 14–15, *15,* 17, 18
Johnson, Robert W. 22–23, 25, 64

K

Kelly, Daisy 3
Kennedy, James 75, 76
King, Billie Jean 89–90, 91, 98, 99,
105
King, Martin Luther, Jr. 66
King, Micki 98
Knapp, Barbara 36
Kormoczy, Suzy 59

L

Ladies Professional Golf
Association (LPGA) 86–87, 100,
110
Lincoln University 44, 46
Llewellyn, Sydney 45–46, 64, 75,
79, 110, 111
Long Island University 75
Louis, Joe 42, 55
LPGA. *See* Ladies Professional Golf
Association (LPGA)

M

Malloy, Gar 92
Marble, Alice 17, 30–31, *32,* 36,
102–103
Mays, Willie 62
McMann, Renville 49
McNeil, Lori 101
Mortimer, Angela 52, 53, 70–71

Muldowney, Shirley 98
Mysterious Five, The 19

N

National Clay Courts
Championships 56, 58
National Lawn Tennis Hall of Fame
95, 111
Navratilova, Martina 98, 102, 105
NCAA (National Collegiate Athletic
Association) 101, 111
New Jersey Governor's Council on
Physical Fitness and Sports 100,
101, 111
New Jersey State Athletic
Commission 111
New York State Open 18
New York Times 26
Nightingale, Gloria 19, 99
Nixon, Richard M. 69
Nyad, Diana 98

O

Olympics, Junior 126
Onorati, Henry 76–77
Orange Lawn Tennis Club 31–32

P

Perry, Bob 49
Peters, Roumania 22

R

Richardson, Ham 49
Robinson, Edna Mae 20, 22
Robinson, Jackie 30, 35, 62, 106
Robinson, Ray "Sugar Ray" 20–22,
21, 62, 75
Rogers, Ginger 36
Roller, Eric 117
Rosenquest, Betty 27
Rubin, Chandra 101

S

Saperstein, Abe 77, 78, 79
Schoenfeld, Bruce 99
Serrill, Juan 13, 14
Smith, Rhoda 15–16, 18–19
Smithsonian Institution 100
Society for the Prevention of
   Cruelty to Children (SPCC) 8, 16
South Carolina Hall of Fame 100,
   111, 130
Sporting News, The 91
Sports Illustrated 101
"Stars of Tennis" tour 90
State Department, U. S. 49, 110
Superstars (TV program) 98–99

T

Theodore Roosevelt Award
   ("Teddy") 101, 111
Tip Top Bread 81, 86, 88
Truman, Christine 59
Tyus, Wyomia 98–99

U

U.S. National Tennis Championship
   26
      1950 33, 109
      1954 44
      1955 47
      1957 69, 110
      1958 73
      See also Forest Hills tourna-
         ment; U.S. Open
U.S. Open
      1971 94–95
      2002 103
      See also Forest Hills tourna-
         ment; U.S. National Tennis
         Championship

United States Lawn Tennis
   Association (USLTA) 26–27, 28,
   30, 31, 38, 41, 43, 64

V

Volpe, Jerry 84

W

Wagner, Robert 66
Walker, Buddy 11, 13, 63
Ward, Pat 57
Ward Baking Company 81, 86, 88
Washington, Sally 2, 6
Washington Generals 78
Weir, Reginald 38
West Side Country Club (Queens,
   NY) 35
Wightman Cup 58, 69–70
Williams, Serena 101, 105
Williams, Venus 72, 101, 105
Wimbledon Tournament
      1951 41–43, 110
      1956 53–56, 58
      1957 58–66, 106, 110
      1958 70–72, 110
      1975 72
      1990 72, 102
      2000 72
      earnings at 120
      Gibson's trophies from
         100–101
      importance of 41
Women's Pro Singles award 78
Women's Tennis Association 105
World Tennis Magazine 56

ABOUT THE AUTHOR

Michael Benson has written biographies for children about Dale Earnhardt, Ronald Reagan, Bill Clinton, William Howard Taft, Malcolm X, Muhammad Ali, Hank Aaron, Lance Armstrong, Jeff Gordon, Wayne Gretzky, and Gloria Estefan. He also edited *All-Time Baseball Greats* and *Fight Game* magazines and is the author of more than 30 books. Originally from Rochester, New York, he is a graduate of Hofstra University. He enjoys his life with his wife and two children in Brooklyn, New York. His goal is to one day write the Great American Novel.

The author wishes to thank the following individuals and organizations for their help: James Chambers, Jake Elwell, Vanessa Nittoli, Neil Romanosky, Howard University, the International Tennis Hall of Fame, and The Brooklyn Public Library.